M.

GW00645001

'6

BREATH WAS THE FIRST DRUMMER

A Treatise on Drums
Drumming and Drummers

Street Musicians, Pencil on art board, Don Gibbins, 10″ x 12″,
1949.

Dedicated to E.J. Gold

Dru Kristel, Nevada City, 1982.

BREATH WAS THE FIRST DRUMMER

DRU KRISTEL

QX Publications/A.D.A.M. Inc.

Cover: *The Light of Sound*, photograph, D. Kristel, 1988.

Copyright © 1995 by Dru Kristel
All Rights Reserved. Printed in the U.S.A.
First Printing.

Published by:
QX Publications/A.D.A.M. Inc.
PO Box 8415, Santa Fe, NM 87504, (505) 982-3402.

No part of this publication may be reproduced or transmitted in any form or by any means, electronic or mechanical, including photocopy, recording, or any information storage and retrieval system now known or to be invented, without permission in writing from the copyright holder, except by a reviewer who wishes to quote brief passages in connection with a review written for inclusion in a magazine, newspaper, or broadcast.
Some of the material in this book first appeared in *The Way of the One Note*, ©1994 and *A Brief History of Music*, ©1994.

Typesetting and design by Sunny Smyth

ISBN: 0-9647845-0-5
Library of Congress Catalog Card Number: 95-79033

TABLE OF CONTENTS

Medicine Pipe Song

Sacred
Pipe of Red Stone
Facing East This Pipe is in My Hand
In My Hand This Pipe of New Beginning
Pipe of Renewal
Red Medicine in My Hand

Sacred
Pipe of Red Stone
Facing South This Plant is in My Hand
In My Hand This Plant of Yellow Healing
Pipe of Healing
Yellow Medicine in My Hand

Sacred
Pipe of Red Stone
Facing West This Flame is in My Hand
In My Hand This Flame of Black Releasing
Pipe of Native Nothingness
Black Medicine in My Hand

Sacred
Pipe of Red Stone
Facing North This Air is in My Hand
In My Hand This Air of White Purity
Pipe of Empowerment
White Medicine In My Hand

Sacred
Pipe of Red Stone
Facing Below and Above
  This Prayer is in My Hand
In My Heart This Prayer of Pure Spirit
Pipe of Prayer Fire
Clear Medicine in My Hand

—M. Silverwolf

Abstract #3, photograph, D. Kristel, 1994.

PREFACE

I knew upon being asked to write a book on the drum that I would not be able to do so without getting into the realm of sound and I cannot very well get into the whole subject of sound without pretty much getting into the whole thing called "Creation".

I was right; it was a setup.

So, here we are and if this is the only book you have on the subject of the drum, drumming or physics, I do not know what to tell you. I would hope that even this book will take you all the way. But really it is being written to add to all of the existing knowledge about such things and is focused around presenting another way in which to view what we already know.

Dru Kristel
May, 1995

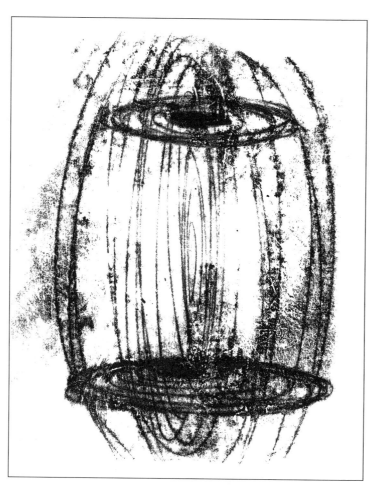

Invisible Barrel Drum, monotype, D. Kristel, 1994.

Chapter One

A BRIEF HISTORY OF MUSIC

Wind was the First Instrument

Man did not invent music. Music was already in Nature. Motion gives arising to all sound. The motion of the wind. The motion of the waters. The motion of the stones. The motion in the fire. The wind alone is an entire orchestra.

The motion of the body, all of its internal noises. Music is a mirror we hold up to ourselves. In it we see reflected everything we have ever experienced. We see the world around us. We see ourselves. We can see how we listen. We can see how we pay attention. We experience presence. We can see how we make love. We see how we evolve. We can see how we dance. Dance in a circle, the shape of the drum, the shape of the world.

The first drum, the human body, with its senses and its rhythms, then the world, with its endless variety of sounds and rhythms. Lightning-flash, winds blowing and the rain drops falling into a small pool. The senses sense nature, and have their arising from that very nature that they are sensing. Nature's way of realizing itself. And yet what is it that is actually experiencing the sensing? The listener; did this consciousness come from nature too? A way to sense the sensing?

The Earth has taught us all we know about music. It has given us its music. It gives us the tools to make its music. In every sound there is music. Visitors from space bring the earth new songs. They come as beautiful stones of every kind.

The universe and the earth make love in this way and they sing together. They have taught us their song in this way. The scratching cicada is the sound of the medicine rattle and our hearts drum out the rhythm as we are giving thanks through appreciation for life itself.

In this way we have learned to play the drum. In this way we have learned to sing, dance and make love. It is all a response, a response to life and being alive in the world. It is the song our parents want us to sing. It is the dance our parents dance. They have taught us this out of love. We are in love when we play music and when we dance. This makes everyone happy. Being in love this way reminds us of our source and there is great joy. The music flows like a flag in the wind and the dance is like that of birds or deer. We play this music and the world listens, impartially, for to nature, it is just another passage in an endless stream of music. For nature, the entire universe is its symphony, its orchestra and its audience.

Nature taught us to turn our mouths into drums. It taught us to put a string on a bent stick. It taught us to put the two together and make the first instrument. But we wanted to share our music with the world and the people so nature taught us to make the drum and with it, make every other kind of instrument. The world is full of every kind of instrument that has its birth in the line of a bowed string and a drum.

We noticed that when we are working together there are rhythms to it. Drum rhythms come up out of life's rhythms and out of working rhythms. When we play music we are facing the eternal. The music is the song of the eternal. The music is the eternal. All of our music comes from vibrations emanating from around a still point, vibrating with, dancing with, in response to an endless nonphenomenal point.

All music comes from stillness. All different sounds have their limit by which they get their name, their sound. Sound is going on all the time, only punctuated by our music and our dance, the rest being open space, undisturbed. Our music is disturbing. We realize that it seems to have an effect not only on ourselves but on the world as well. We put bowed strings on barrels and even half barrels and reduced the drumming motion of the hands to tiny butterfly movements to be disturbing, to influence the world and ourselves.

Breathing was the first drummer and everything flows out of it. The rhythms of life reflected in our music. Pygmy choirs in excellence. The rhythms of life finely woven together with such naturalness. Music is a form of gratitude. And sometimes our music appears to us as the healing one. Our music is in everything we do and our life is music. And sometimes we dance with the music. Dancing is a way to show our appreciation, and our presence in the world, as part of the world and its eternal dance with the sun and with the universe.

The universe is full of instruments for disturbing stillness and our music is one of them. This is why we make music in a sacred way.

Now the world is full of instruments and there is less and less music. Less and less beauty. We need to be able to play this music again and dance and work and move with the rhythms of life. There is a tendency toward mechanicality the farther one is from the source of the music. When the instrument disappears where does the music go?

Back to the same place it came from, to do all over again. This is one rhythm of the universe, only one among the multitude. We, each of us, used to come together with our voices and our drums and weave intricate patterns that our parents taught us, into songs about the world and about the universe.

The rocks and stones taught us their songs and the water taught us the way in which to play them. The fire taught us the dances and the wind taught us to soar with the music, like the air itself. Each taught us something about how to move around in the universe and each is giving a part of itself to us as we play the music of life.

I know this may not seem like much of a history lesson on drums but this is what the universe and the world taught us to do and we love doing it. This is what we have done with it, and this is what we are doing with it.

Fixed Aperture Photograph, D. Kristel, 1993.

A Very Old Work Song

Ho-a-a, Ho-a-a, Heiti-na, Heiti-na
Motatza Shiuana Kopishtai, Guatzena
Sa Uashtany-i, Sa Nashtio
Sa Uishe, Sa Ahtzeta, Raua
Opona, Opona, Opona Motatza
Uakany-i, Maseua, Hotshany-i Chayan
To Ima Satyumisha Shashka, Shipapu
Ho-a-a, Ho-a-a, Heiti-na, Heiti-na.

My friend, Spirit entity, Greetings
My sacrificial bowl, My father
My child, My scalp, Is good
Come in, Come in, Come in, My friend
War magician, Great Spirit, Transit guide
Come here my brother,
Road runner of the Space between worlds.

—M. Silverwolf

A series of monotypes depicting the sound
of a gong, D. Kristel, 1994.

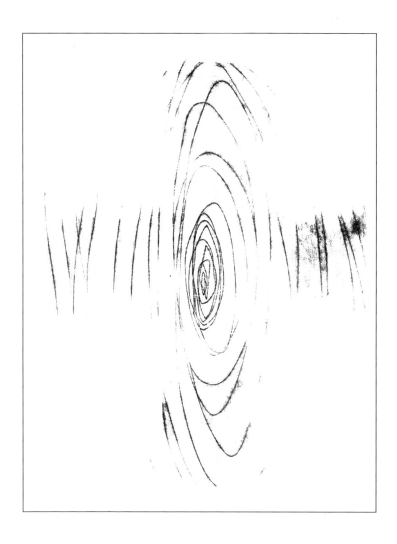

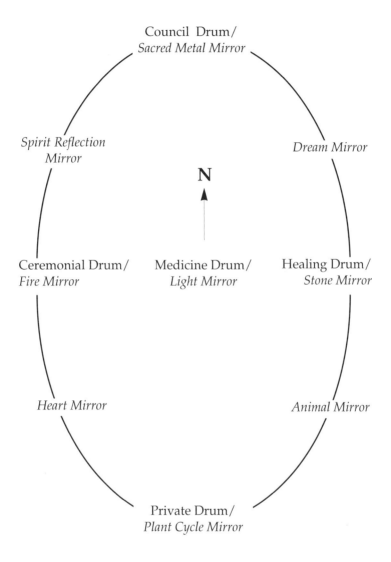

Council Drum/
Sacred Metal Mirror

*Spirit Reflection
Mirror*

Dream Mirror

N

Ceremonial Drum/
Fire Mirror

Medicine Drum/
Light Mirror

Healing Drum/
Stone Mirror

Heart Mirror

Animal Mirror

Private Drum/
Plant Cycle Mirror

Excerpted from *The Great Sweet Medicine Wheel* by Dru Kristel,
QX Publications, 1993.

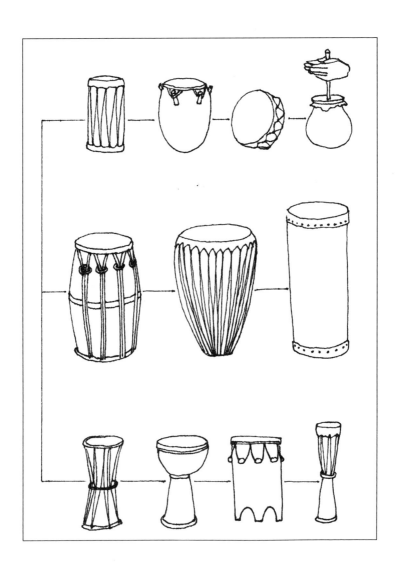

Chapter Two

A BRIEF PICTORIAL HISTORY OF THE DRUM

Membranophones Classified by Shape

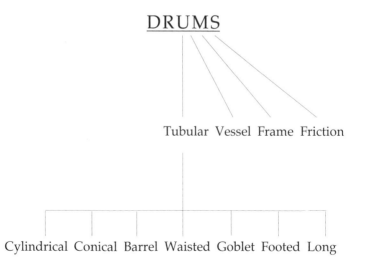

DRUMS

Tubular Vessel Frame Friction

Cylindrical Conical Barrel Waisted Goblet Footed Long

African Djembé with bottle top shaker, photograph,
D. Kristel, 1994.

Chapter Three

DRUM TYPES

Drums have been made in all shapes and sizes and are made out of anything you can think of. Partially this is because they appear to be an easy target sound-wise. After all, to play a drum, you just hit it and take your chances. No?

In this chapter we are going to take a look at the wide variety of drums and other percussive instruments. Notice that I am already separating drums from other types of percussive tools, separating the "waters from the waters", so to speak. Sometimes these "waters" become pretty cloudy in terms of what is a drum and what is not. And as long as we are at it, let us put a little distance between the "percussionist" and the "drummer". These two have been sharing the same room for a very long time. They may be cousins, but still keep in mind, they are from two different families.

Now when it comes to drums in particular, there is a simple guideline that we can follow as to the why and the wherefore of their differing shapes. It goes like this:

Longer	*will make a*	Shorter
Bigger	*deeper sound than....*	Smaller
Thicker		Thinner
More dense		Less dense
Heavier		Lighter
Relaxed		Tense
Slower		Faster
Looser		Tighter
Softer		Harder

Variation in any of the factors listed will produce a different pitch. For instance, just in the drum head itself, the tone of the drum it is stretched on will vary according to the head's size, as well as how it is played. The tone and pitch of the head can vary widely depending on where it is struck and with what. There is also the fact that some drum heads are made up of multiple layers of membrane sandwiched together and sometimes have things attached to them, such as, a spot of chapati paste, a wheat flour paste mixed with iron powder, applied to the drumhead slightly wet, and flattened out into a spot about two or three inches in diameter. When this dries, it sticks to the head and effectively lowers the pitch as well as increasing the sustain, or ringing quality of the drum. You will notice these kinds of spots, especially on the drums from India; the tabla and the mridangam.

Other major factors then, would be the diameter, length and thickness of the drum's shell or body, variations in the shell through combinations of shapes, and whether or not something other than chapati paste has been affixed to the drum head or the shell of the drum. Some examples of this would be a sympathetic string which rings when the drum is tuned properly creating a type of droning sound, or perhaps a spider's web placed over the mouth or open end of the drum producing a buzzing sound like that of a kazoo.

So far we have been looking at drums with only one head and a single shell. But what about drums which have a head at both ends and/or are made up of two or more shells?

Drums with heads at both ends are known as membranophones (actually, all drums with a drum head on either one or both ends are called membranophones) and the distance between the heads can be either a few inches or a few feet. The purpose in putting a second head on a drum is to lower the tone and amplify the first head. Both heads certainly influence each other and are usually matching in size and weight. A good example of this type of drum is the double-sided Native American hoop drum. Another example would be the kaido drums of Japan.

Sometimes the two heads on one drum will be of different sizes and are tuned relative to each other. These types of drum are always barrel-shaped, tapered gradually from the low end to the high end. An example of this type of drum is the East Indian mridangam, which, as time went on, was neatly cut in half and turned into the first tabla/bayan drum sets. The tabla/bayan are found all through India and the Middle East but vary greatly as to how they are played and how they are made. Tabla/bayan come in different sizes and are made of wood for the tabla drum and ceramic, metal and sometimes wood for the bayan drum.

The most common examples of drums composed of multiple heads and shells are bongo, conga and tabla. In this case, we are talking about two or more separate drums grouped together and referred to by the name of the soprano or high pitched lead drum of the set. For instance, "the tabla" refers to the set of two drums, although the tabla is actually the small high end drum and the bayan is the large low end drum played with the other hand. The same is true for the set of drums called "the conga". The actual conga in this case is the mid-range drum in a set of three drums that go by the names of quinta, conga and tumba; small, medium and large.

A really interesting fact worth mentioning at this point is that most drums receive their names by the sound that they make. In other words, drums tend to name themselves by the sounds they make. If you know how these different drums sound you can easily hear the similarity in their name. Go ahead and try it with the words quinta, conga and tumba; I will wait.

Using the East Indian tabla set, say the word tabla and in it you can hear the basic sounds that the drum produces. Now try bayan; again, you can hear the basic sounds that the drum produces, even the slurred pitch it makes as the heel of the hand varies the tension on the head, raising and lowering the tuning.

Speaking of raising and lowering the tuning and the pitch of drums while being played, which can be done using the hands, sticks and pads, we must take a look at the most common type of drum which gets its generic name from its ability to jump and slide around within an entire octave of notes. This type of drum is referred to as a talking drum. Found throughout Latin America, Africa, India, China and Japan, these drums can not only produce a wide range of notes from a single playing head, but also give glissandos and other special effects when in the hands of a virtuoso.

Talking drums are almost always hourglass-shaped with cording or leather thongs stretched from the rim of one drumhead to the other. By squeezing these thongs with the hand or between one arm and the body, the musician can increase or decrease the tension of the heads. The exact shape of the hourglass body of the drum may vary from the dundun and gangan of Ghana to the udukkai of

Kerala, India, or the chang go, which is the national drum of Korea, but the basic principle for playing them remains the same.

These days, drums are made of every available material including PVC tubing, mylar plastics and nylon rope. These substances, while perhaps lacking in esthetic, can be a real boon to the percussionist. They tend to be very tough and they are not subject to the influences of humidity and temperature as are the natural woods and animal skins used in the making of most older indigenous drums. They also offer an alternative to those who are squeamish about handling dead animal parts. It is important to mention here though, that in the aboriginal mind-set, it is considered a fact that the spirit of the animal whose parts are being used to make the drum, dwells in that drum, and part of the voice of the drum is the sound of that animal's spirit. This is why in some cultures the drums are kept in a special house of their own, and are shown great respect through their care and maintenance including offerings of food, incense and special songs. In one village in Africa, they go so far as raising the cattle that will be used for making the rawhide drumheads separately from the rest of the herd and when these drums are not being played for ceremonies and sacred dances, they are handled only by select young girls—virgins, of course.

I mention this to demonstrate a point of view— that is, the intimate relationship that exists between the musician, the instrument, and the community of which they are a part. In most cultures there is a deep, intimate connection between the shaman and his tools. The tools are considered an extension of the one to whom they belong. These music tools are handed down through the generations and are highly respected for their connection to their previous owners and therefore are shown the same respect that would be shown to the people themselves. Often times these tools are buried and forgotten for lack of anyone to pass them on to and this connection is purposely broken.

This simple factor explains why some objects and drums in particular, receive the kind of treatment that they do. It is true that "you get out of a thing what you put into it", and this kind of music certainly transcends the strictly recreational aspect and clearly demonstrates why it is that certain drums seem to have an almost overwhelming effect not only on the musician but on all those within range of their sound.

As I mentioned earlier, there is a difference between drummers and percussionists. A drummer usually plays a drum or drums, whereas a percussionist not only plays drums but is also skilled in the playing of a wide range of percussive instruments. Even in a western style orchestra we have our drummers, those who primarily play the tympany, snare and bass drum, and then we have percussionists who handle the parts calling for bells, xylophone, woodblocks, tubular bells, glockenspiel, cymbals and triangle.

And last but certainly not least, we have the trap set. The traps, short for contraption, is a generic term used to refer to a collection of drums and percussion accessories including cymbals. Trap sets are usually made up of a bass drum played with the foot using a pedal with a mallet attached to it. The mallet can be either wooden or compressed felt. Another drum in the set is the snare drum, so called because of the strings, wires or snares that are strung tightly across the surface of the bottom head giving this drum its unusual high pitched sound. The rest of the set is composed of one or more tom-tom drums of different sizes and tunings and one or more floor toms of different sizes and tunings to provide for the low end. The other foot takes up the hi-hat, which is a stand with a pedal affixed at the bottom and a shaft leading up to a pair of small cymbals at the top of the stand which separate and come together as the foot is raised and lowered. The hi-hat is truly unique to the traps and demonstrates the ingenuity of its progenitors. This arrangement, then, covers a whole spectrum of tuned drums and cymbals which can be played by only one person.

I am sure we are all familiar with the trap set through its use in jazz and rock music, even though the traps are the new kids on the block. The trap drums are not only unique in their construction but also in how they are played. Each trap drummer is required to be virtually a one man band of percussive sounds, and this demands of him being able to split his attention evenly between both feet and both hands as well as the music of which he is a part. This alone is a skill in itself not found among most percussionists and usually takes years of training to develop. It is this factor, I think, which lends itself to the common results of most trap drummers being not only talented in splitting their attention (which can manifest as "spaced out"), but also being regular right brain, left brain wizards. It is worth noting here, too, that the majority of trap drummers are so encoded in their muscles that they make terrible dancers. The patterns of their dance are very different from the twist, the frug and the monkey. However, they begin to get close to fitting in when it is time for the watusi and other forms of organic, essence-type dancing.

Now, if we look at how drums are actually played, whether with sticks or with the hands, we have a pretty good picture of how all the different sound qualities in drumming are produced.

Let us start with the hands. The key to drumming is in the hands even if sticks are used. With some drums, such as the conga, the whole of both hands are used when playing. Contrast this with the dumbek drum in which only the fingers are used to attain all of the different sounds. The tabla/bayan drums land half way between these two extremes, using both the fingers and the palm of the hands to make the incredible range of tones as well as tuning.

The essence of technique with the hands is to minimalize the amount of motion required to produce the sound and patterns. In other words, the less force spent on producing the tones, the more force to spend on precision and endurance. Likewise, the longer the stroke, the longer the time spent between strokes. So, for speed, compression of movement is the key.

Sticks are used extensively throughout the world for playing drums. However, the sticks are just extensions of the hand's ability to keep rhythms. In snare drumming, the essence of the technique is to reduce all of the movements required to control the sticks, down to just the fingers, so that there is very little motion (or time) spent on having to move the arms, wrists and hands. The same principle applies also to the dumbek and tabla drums mentioned earlier.

Sticks vary greatly in size and shape. Each type of drum stick will produce a different sound from the same drum. Drums and the sticks they are played with, have been grouped together in favorite combinations, but it is highly recommended to experiment around to discover new sounds through playing the same drum in different ways. You will find a handy wood block right there on the side of every drum. Go ahead and use it.

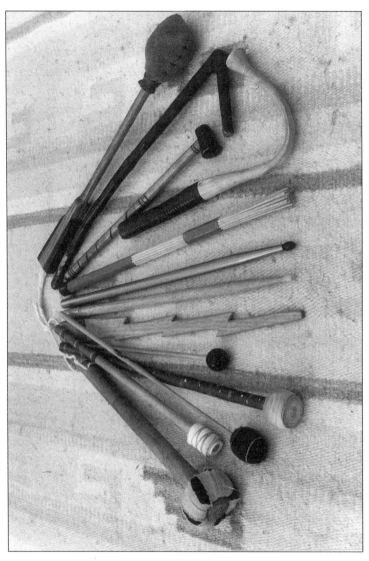

Photograph, D. Kristel, 1994.

Sound 18, monotype, D. Kristel, 1994.

Chapter Four

TUNING DRUMS

Tuning is probably the most underrated and overlooked aspect of drums and drumming. Generally drums are tuned to the individual piece of music being performed. If the drums are soloing, they are tuned to themselves. Drums are always tuned relative to their size and shape. In the case of a single-headed instrument, the head is tuned in relationship to the shell that it is on so that the resonate qualities of both reinforce each other. This is the pitch aspect of tuning. Tuning the head itself is done by going around the outside edge of the head near the rim while tapping lightly with the fingers or a stick and adjusting the tension of the head every inch or so until it rings with a consistent tone without any vibrato or dissonant harmonics.

Tuning the head is prerequisite to establishing the pitch. Once the head is tuned within itself the pitch can then be raised using tension or heat, and the tuning will remain consistent.

Tension is produced by using either tight straps or threaded rods connecting the rim of the head and the shell of the drum. Heat is produced by a flame or the heat of the body. The sun makes a great heat source and occasionally I have been known to place my tabla/bayan on or around the old fashioned steam-heater a half an hour or so before a class.

Most drums, especially those with animal skin heads, are kept on the loose side for storage or when not being played. This prevents them from getting too tight through temperature changes and lack of humidity. Too much tightness can result in damage to the heads and even the shell, which can be crushed under the extreme pressure exerted by some types of heavier rawhide.

Humidity affects natural heads in the extreme; therefore, most drums should be kept in a cool, dry place. Lack of playing also effects drums radically. The very lack of stretching and limbering as a result of being tuned and played results in a stiffening and hardening of the heads and does not allow the heads to readjust themselves on the shell. This is why, occasionally after a long storage, a drum will make a "poing" sound as though it has been struck. This is the sound of the head unsticking itself from the shell and from the drum's point of view, is a huge relief. In its extreme form, this kind of sticking and pulling results in a torn head.

With heads made of mylar none of these conditions are concern for worry. However, if an outdoor concert is in the works, be sure you and your drum are in the shade—they do melt.

Water drums of all kinds are tuned by the amount of water used in the shell and how wet the heads are kept while being played. Water, which is a great amplifier, also makes it possible to adjust the pitch while being played by rocking the water within the drum. The Native American view of the water drum is that the water in the drum and the water in the human body vibrate together through sympathetic resonance and on occasion, the water from the drum will be used ceremonially after it has been charged up with all those vibrations.

In the case of double-headed drums, the two heads are tuned relative to each other, either in harmonic intervals or the same exact note and pitch.

When a drum is properly tuned, there will be a consistent tone without vibrato throughout the entire diminishing of the ringing sound produced. If not, you will hear two or more tones which are easy to distinguish when going around the rim slowly tapping. By either raising the low note to match the higher note or by bringing the higher note down to the lower note, you should be able to go all the way around the rim of the head getting the same tone and be able to strike the drum from any side and get a consistent tone that rings clearly and is not flat.

I cannot stress enough the value of drum cases and/or a cabinet to keep drums in, especially for sensitive hand drums such as the tabla, dumbek and hoop drums. A good case will not only keep dust off your drums, but also buffer against sudden temperature and humidity changes.

Whenever you are warming up a drum, by whatever means, never leave it unattended, thus avoiding breakage. Many percussionists believe that the attention and adoration that they place on their instruments at this time affects the whole atmosphere of the music—"brings it to life", so to speak.

So far we have been looking at drums that are round. What about drums that are square, hexagonal and so on? Here we have a world of drums as diverse as the history of the world.

Basically, whatever you can stretch a membrane onto has sufficed as the body of a drum at some point on this planet. Sometimes just the membrane itself is inflated and used as a drum like hitting a balloon. The Lena Lanape people of North America simply used a moist piece of raw hide, usually the whole hide, folded around a core of sticks piled together lengthwise and allowed to dry and harden, pulling tight around the sticks.

On occasion, a deep hole is dug into the earth and a piece of wet rawhide is staked down over the hole and allowed to dry and stretch tight, making for a perfect big drum that you do not have to carry with you. Another example of this is found in Alaska, where one of the favorite drums is the walrus stomach hoop drum. These are some of the most beautiful drums in the world. The sound quality of this super thin rawhide, combined with its short drying time, make it the perfect thing, especially for those long "medicine-walks". Neatly folded up into a package the size of a small wallet and dried, the walrus stomach carries easily and when you get to where you are going, if you haven't brought your folded up rim with you, take a nice sapling and split it into two pieces lengthwise, wet the rawhide for a few minutes, bend half of the sapling wood into the right sized hoop, stretch the rawhide over the hoop, and with that string you remembered to bring along, tie the head onto the rim around the outside edge. Now with a little help from your sacred fire, you can slowly dry and tighten up your drum and stay warm for a full night of drumming.

The Native American cottonwood drums of the Southwest are great examples of oddly shaped drums and the ability of rawhide to take any contour. These drums are famous for their sound even though they are seldom very round—their makers taking full advantage of the trees' natural size and shape.

Another favorite stand-in for a drum frame has been the wooden packing box. These are usually square and occasionally rectangular, made of hardwood and definitely work in a pinch. The real drawback with square drums is that if they are tied up too tightly the sides of the shell bow in towards the center affecting not only the tone of the drum, but also making it difficult to get any high pitched sounds. The other aspect of all square drums is their tuning, in that there are different lengths across the head, from center to the straight sides of the rim and from center to the corners and everything in between. This makes for a whole range of tones on a single head and harmonic qualities that are not to be found in round drums.

The Moroccan drummers use a small square drum with matching heads about two inches apart that has a snare drum sound to it when a single snare is drawn tightly over one of the heads and is played with the fingers. They use this drum mostly as accompaniment to a series of exercises using a chain laden bar as a weight.

Having built and played many square drums over the last ten years, it has been very rewarding and inspirational in terms of the harmonic and polytonal potential that square and rectangular drums have to offer. The major users of square drums are to be found in Tibet, the Middle East and in North and South America.

There have been drums made using four human femur bones tied together to form a square drum frame and there are many drums made taking advantage of the natural resonating qualities of the human skull, either as a whole, or more popularly, just the top portion is used and two of these are affixed together forming two bowls with goat skin stretched over their openings. To this are added two thongs with beads on the ends and a handle or sash connected in the middle between the two bowls, allowing the player to rotate and spin the drum with one hand. Not always made of skull bones, these types of drums are known as "damaru", and are found all around the world.

Years ago I had the great fortune of having an exquisite skull bone damaru from Tibet which, alas, was eaten by a friend's dog, Puppy. Upon arriving home to see just the end of the drum's tassel peeking out of Puppy's mouth like the tip of her tongue, my friend seemed even more shocked by the response this elicited from myself and another friend. When we burst out laughing at the whole scene, Puppy's owner didn't appear amused and informed us that he didn't get the joke. We then told him that it seemed a perfect and fitting end for a damaru of that type. After all, the drum and how it is made addresses the whole issue of the transient nature of life itself. And then we told him to keep an eye on Puppy, for more than just health reasons.

Turtle shells have long been used as drum shells, and so have gourds and seashells. But the all time first place has to go to the family of drums that are made of one or more heads stretched onto a ceramic shell or bowl.

Unlike having to stretch a skin over an uneven shape, the ceramic shells gave the drum makers the

combination of shape, size and resonance. And if
you are in an area where big trees or lots of wood
are not around for making drums, the ceramic shell
is the answer to all your drum-making problems.

Occasionally people have gone so far as to
carve drum shells out of stone such as marble, jade,
granite, lava, limestone, gypsum and basalt. These
come in all shapes and sizes and sometimes use
water as an amplifier and tuning device. There was
a very famous drum in China which belonged to
the Empress. This tiny drum was carved in the
finest jade inlaid with gold and was so delicate that
it actually produced a low tone of considerable volume.

This brings us to the most significant influence
on a drum's tone, pitch and volume, next to the
drum shell itself. It is the drum head or heads and
whether or not they have been made with anything
that will take the stretch or shrink and harden.

Along with walrus stomach, goat skin and cow
hide, the most widely used types of skin are snake
and fish. The thinner the membrane, the more extreme the tuning potential of the drum it is on. A
thin membrane can make a small diameter drum
sound large and a large drum ring clearly with high
notes close to the rim.

The thicker the membrane, the more dull the
tone becomes and the drums will respond with less
of a bell quality. The Kaido drums of Japan are an
excellent example of the master craftsmanship and

critical precision involved in making drums this large that ring the way these drums do.

Once we get into drum shells with more than four sides, the more they resemble round drums with all of the same qualities as those found in the round drum family.

Photograph, D. Kristel, 1988.
Credit: Hide & Seek Drum Company.

Frequency Patterns in Various Media
Images by D. Kristel, 1994.

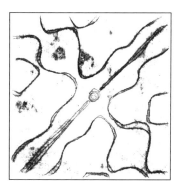

Single Note on a Plate/
Low Intensity

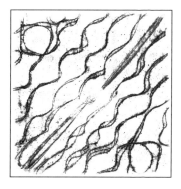

Single Note on a Plate/
High Intensity

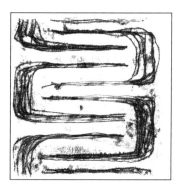

Single Note Wave Pattern
in Magnetic Field

Single Note Wave Pattern
in Magnetic Field

Two Notes Impacting
in Viscous Liquid

Two Notes Impacting in
Viscous Liquid

Two Notes Impacting/
Third Wave Pattern

Two Notes Impacting/
Third Wave Pattern

Single Note in Liquid/
Low Intensity

Single Note in Liquid/
High Intensity

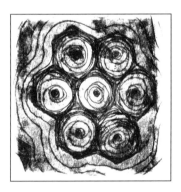

Single Note Wave Pattern
in Liquid

Two Note Wave Pattern
in Liquid

Chapter Five

RIM SHOTS

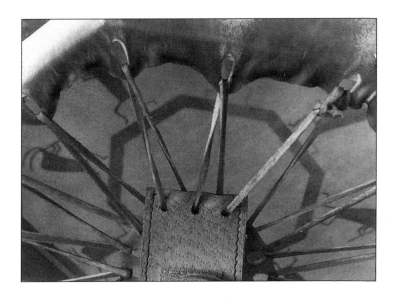

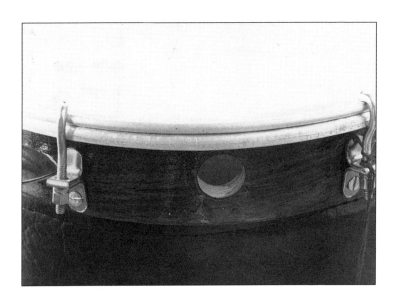

Photo credits for Rim Shots: Coleen Rowe, Santa Fe, 1995.

Ntenga drum from Uganda, photograph, D. Kristel, 1994.

Chapter Six

MAKING DRUMS

We are going to look at making drums of all kinds rather than focusing on a specific type of drum. As a consequence, you may find this information useful in repairing some of the drums you already have or in picking up a broken drum for a song and sprucing it up for that next bongo party or Sufi spin-fest marked on your calendar.

Drums are basically very user-friendly; however, when they do break they are usually set aside as nonoperative, so we will look at how to repair the shells as well as repair or replace the heads.

Let us start at the top. As mentioned earlier, the most common types of drum heads are either rawhide skins of goat, cow, deer and elk. Some are made of fish or snake skin and occasionally even paper, woven nylon or fiberglass can be found. Outside of natural materials, mylar heads are the most common and have worked their way into the drum world on top of almost every type of shell made, so let us start with these.

Mylar heads have been available since the 1950's. I remember the shock when replacing my old goat skin heads that came with my first Slingerland trap set. My only other drum was a marching classical, mahogany snare drum, again with goat skin heads. After years of play the heads began to split and I purchased all new mylar heads to replace them. At first I was very disappointed. That warm full sound was now booming and ringing all over the place and whole ranges of subtle tones were missing. I quickly learned to use dampening devices such as cloth strips under the heads, duct tape, felt, clamp-on adjustable felt pads, rings cut out of construction paper, or old heads, a hankie or even a wallet laid over the top head to control the amount of ring and sustain.

The next surprise in using the new mylar heads came at a "grand-opening" parking lot gig. It was a hot summer weekend and by the end of the first day the drum heads were so badly dented and pitted from the hot sun and hard drumming that I had to rush to the music store for another set of top heads for the next day.

Mylar heads have changed, improved and diversified greatly since then and in some ways have definite advantages over rawhide heads. All mylar heads require some sort of rim and lug-bolt system to affix it to the shell and to control the tuning of the drum. This makes mylar heads very appealing, not only in terms of their tunability but also in how easy they are to buy and replace. You can get mylar heads from any local music store. If not, you can order directly from distributors. Mylar heads come in a variety of sizes and thicknesses. They are also made to be clear, colored, mirrored and multi-layered. You will have to experiment to find the sound you are looking for or hopefully your local music store has drums you can play and hear first hand.

To replace mylar heads, start by loosening the lug-bolts known as "tuning lugs" that connect the rim holding the head to the "side-plates" which are affixed to the shell of the drum itself (See Chapter 5, "Rim Shots"). You can use a typical drum-key or an ordinary ratchet-type wrench that fits the tuning lugs. Never use pliers; they strip the tuning lugs and scratch the shell. My favorite method is to use the ratchet-wrench snap on head on the end of the extension rod clamped into a cordless drill which makes the job really fast and easy. Occasionally, the tuning lugs will have a screw-type head and for this, simply use a screwdriver or a cordless drill with a screwdriver attachment. Fine tuning the head is always done by hand, using the key or screwdriver.

After removing all of the tuning lugs, pull off the rim. If the drum head does not come off with the rim, do not be afraid to pull it off the shell. If you have not already purchased the new head, take the old head with you to the music store to be sure that your new head will fit properly. Mylar heads come in $1/2$ inch increments, so be sure to measure the drum shell diameter very carefully from outside edge to outside edge in the event that you do not have the old head.

Now that you are ready to put on the new head, stop and take a few minutes to inspect the drum shell itself. You want to look for any sharp edges, splinters or loose material on or around the rim as well as inside the shell. These can either ruin your new head or create a lot of buzzing sounds in the drums when you are playing. In the case of loose material, simply brush it out and wipe clean. For splinters or rough edges, take some 150 grit sandpaper and sand them off. Just be careful that you do not distort the shape of the rim. Wipe clean any particles from sanding and you are ready to go!

Start with placing the new head on the shell and be sure that it is centered evenly all the way around. Mylar heads are pre-shaped with a metal edge. Now place the metal rim of the drum down over the metal edge and line up the holes with the sideplates. In the case of rim-hooks, simply hang them in alignment with the side plates also. Thread the bolts into or through the sideplates. Attach the connecting lug-nut to the bolts if you do not have threaded sideplates, but do not tighten them down in either case. You want the rim moveable and ad-justable—firstly, to facilitate lining up the bolts and secondly, you do not want to lop-side or buckle the drum head. This requires tightening them only a few turns each, moving around the rim as you go.

Once all the slack has been taken up in the bolts, check again to be sure you do not have any kinks in the head even though you may see ripples at this stage.

Begin to tighten each lug-bolt only a turn at a time until the head has stretched itself out nice and tight and then you can adjust the tuning (See Chapter 4, "Tuning Drums").

That is about it for mylar heads. When it comes to rawhide heads, it is a whole other bag. The word rawhide means just what it says—we are talking raw animal skins with or without hair. These are usually untreated, scraped to an even thickness, stretched out and left out to dry. The skins or heads are usually a mottled yellow color, if unbleached, and white if bleached chemically. Bleaching usually takes most of the natural oils out of the rawhide, which is what causes the whitening and makes the skins more brittle. This means that the fibers in the skin are more prone to breaking. On the positive side, however, it can make for a more brilliant sounding head. It only means that we have to be a little more careful not to tear the head as we stretch it on the shell when it is wet or pull it too tight, which will cause it to tear upon shrinking as it dries.

That brings up the main point about how to work wet rawhide heads—the shrinkage factor. In this section, we are going to deal with heads that are applied without using any hardware. Some rawhide heads such as tabla/bayan, bongo, conga, etc. can be ordered or purchased through the local music store. They come pre-formed and usually with some sort of ring in them or attached to them, so that you simply use the same techniques as in changing mylar heads; that is, if your drum has metal hardware and is done with dry heads. Never soak these type of heads.

If your drum does not have hardware, then we are going to glue, tie or nail the wet rawhide directly to the shell. Let us say your drum has a broken head. Unless it is wooden, the head has probably been glued on. If it is tied or nailed, the first step will be to soak the head in slightly warm water, and if you are starting from scratch with a piece of rawhide, do the same with it (the bathtub works well for this). This takes about an hour or so, and when the hide is soft, it is ready for you to pull the old head off.

The glue has loosened by now and should just pull right off using the fingers. If there is decorative trim around the head where it meets the shell to cover the glued edge, it just pulls off first. But if you need to, wedge a dull butter knife up between the shell and the edge of the head and gently start working it around the drum.

Once you get the old head off, you now have a template to cut your new head. Scrunch the old head as flat as you can and draw a line around it about a quarter of an inch larger. Cut out the new head using common scissors. With your Elmer's-type white, water-based glue, put an ample amount of glue in an even layer covering the edge of the drum and down the side to at least as far as the rawhide will reach.

Now place your new, wet head centered on the shell and carefully place a long strip of paper masking tape on the diameter so that it crosses the head and bends the edge over the shell, past the rawhide and onto the shell. If the head sags a little, that is okay; but do not let it droop, as it will not dry tightly enough. Do not pull the skin tight either, as this will happen as the skin dries.

Take another long piece of tape and repeat the same move at right angles to the first piece to make a cross. Two more times and you will have an eight spoked wheel. From this point, you can use shorter pieces of tape to fill in the wedges all the way around to hold the edge of rawhide tightly to the shell. You can almost mold the rawhide flat after you get all the tape on, checking for loose or lifted edges. Any glue that smears under the tape can be wiped off with a damp cloth after the head has dried and the tape has all been removed. The tape does not stick to the wet rawhide, but does well to hold the edge and does not usually stick to the glue either. This is nice when you are pulling it off and cleaning up any glue spots. If you are in a pinch, and do not have any masking tape, you can always use rubber bands, bungee-cord, rope or cloth strips to tie around the edge to hold down the rawhide. But this is not easy to do, and you want to work quickly so that your glue does not dry or the head begins to shrink before you are finished. This process usually only takes about 45 minutes; but if the head begins to dry out a bit, take a wet sponge and dampen what rawhide you can.

I usually leave the drum to sit for 18 to 24 hours with the tape on. The moisture in the rawhide slows the glue drying, and the tape slows the rawhide drying time, so that the glue has dried before the head starts to really shrink, which it does very well. When pulling off the tape, do so gently, so as to avoid lifting up the rawhide. If you do, or you find a spot that is not stuck well and lifts up a little, just work some fresh glue on a stick under the edge and retape.

Allow 48 to 72 hours for the new head to really shrink all the way and you will now know how your drum is going to sound. At this point, if you see a slump or sag in the head, or if it is too tight, soak and redo. You can glue the old or new trim into place using the same water-based glue. Trims are usually cloth, rope, or leather, and give the drum a finishing touch. They also serve to protect the edge of the head from getting snagged and pulled up.

In the case of the wooden shells, taping is unnecessary. Instead, use little nails called brads, upholstery nails or thumbtacks to hold the edge of the rawhide down. Use as many as you need; these are left after the head dries and are covered by the trim, which can either be just glued on or held in place using decorative small nails or tacks long enough to go through the trim, the rawhide and into the shell.

So far we have been assuming that everything is working out just fine with the new head—but what if it is not? Let us take a few minutes at this point to troubleshoot some of the possible things that could have gone wrong and what to do about them.

Remember, the thing that makes wet rawhide work is the shrinkage. At first, we do not know what to expect: "Is this too tight? Is this too loose?" With dry rawhide heads using metal hardware, it is easy—just tighten or loosen until it is right, so if you want to change the tuning, it is simple.

When it comes to trying to predict just how far the rawhide will shrink, experience alone is the greatest teacher. Here are some basic guidelines that will help get you started. Cow and goat skins shrink more than deer or elk. They are also harder and more prone to tearing. Deer and elk skins are softer, more supple and much more malleable. They take to being pulled a little tighter.

When you are finished "tying-up" your drum, the wet rawhide should remind you of a soft pita bread! It should be loose, but not droopy, and just slightly concave. Make sure there are no wedge-shaped dips when you look across the head's surface. If so, then this can be corrected by pulling the rawhide slightly tighter at right angles to the slump; that is, if the slump runs from your left to right, pull the head tighter toward and away from yourself, and reattach it to the shell.

If the rawhide is too tightly drawn on the shell or frame, besides tearing the head, you run the risk of warping the frame out of shape or, in the case of ceramic shells, the heads will actually crack the shell. I have even seen the whole rim of the shell ripped right off along with the head. If this happens, there is no way to repair the shell other than grinding the shell down to form a new rim. Sometimes this works, but you definitely have a new drum and a new head size.

A rule of thumb in drum making, until you have the hands-on experience, is this: It is better to have the head come out too loose and redo it, than to have to replace the head or the shell itself.

The other techniques used in working wet rawhide heads are to tie them on to the shell. This can be done using wet rawhide strips about 1/4 to 1/2 inch in width. It is also possible to use rope, cord, or even tough string. This depends on how big your drum is and the look that you want it to have. When using cord to tie up with, the head has to be pulled slightly tighter than with rawhide strips, which also shrink upon drying.

There are three basic styles of tying up. The first is to simply punch a hole about an inch in from the very edge of the rawhide, which will overhang the shell. The holes should be about an inch apart all the way around for small to medium-sized drums. Drums larger in diameter than 12 inches can tolerate holes as far apart as two inches. To punch the holes, a standard paper punch from the stationary department works great. If the skin is really thick cowhide, you may need to purchase a hole punch from the local leather working store or make your own by sharpening the inside edge of a piece of small pipe. Lay the wet skin over a piece of wood and hit the pipe through with a hammer. Never just cut a slit in the skin with a knife, as these invariably tear.

After punching the holes, center the head, or heads (in the case of double-headed drums), and feed the end of the rawhide strip cut to a point through one of the holes. Pull about six inches through and tie this short end off using a simple half square knot or a slip knot. You need this end to tie the final knot when you have laced the drum all the way around.

If you are doing double heads, feed the lacing through the matching hole on the bottom head. It works best if you feed the lacing from the shell side of the hole outward and pull it through the hole slowly and carefully. This is where most tears happen. You do not want a lot of slack in the lacing, but do not try to pull it tight at this time. Continue going back and forth between heads until you come to where you started. This gives you a nice "V" pattern on the side of your drum. If you want a crisscross pattern, then feed the lacing straight down to the bottom head and work it back in the opposite direction, crossing the first set of lacings until you return to where you started. In either case, you can then begin from where you first tied the lacing to the first head and begin taking up the slack from the tie-up. Do not just pull down on the lacing, but rather pull the lacing through each hole by pulling up and out, thus avoiding tearing.

Single-sided hoop drum of deerskin, 14″ diameter, photograph, D. Kristel, 1994.

If you are tying up a single-headed drum, the technique is the same as above; the difference being, to what do you tie onto if not another head? If you are tying up a hoop-type drum, it is easy. Loop the lacing around the back of the rim through the opposite hole in the head and back again to the hole next to the one you started with. Alternate your way back and forth around the shell until you are back to where you started, through that hole, and then begin to pull the slack out of the lacing. When you finish this, feed the lacing to the center of the back of the drum to where all of the lacings cross over one another. Take the lacing around the cluster of laces and pull them together. It may take several times around the center point to get them all together and centered. Now start weaving the lacing over and under the spokes and pull tight as you go until your run out of lacing or have a palm-sized circle. This makes a great handhold, and can even be covered with cloth.

If you are tying up a shell that is dumbek in shape, that is, a bowl on top of a cylinder, use the same technique as the hoop drum. Just go around the cylinder where it meets the bottom of the bowl, and tie the lacing off where you started.

If you are tying up a straight cylinder, there are several options available. The easiest is to use the hoop drum technique; otherwise, some sort of hardware has to be used. This can be pegs or rigid hoops, but these must be affixed to the shell, which involves drilling. With wooden drum shells this is not a problem; however, pegs and ceramics do not mix.

Let us look at wooden shells first. The quickest method is to simply drill $3/16$ inch holes in the shell an inch or so below where the holes in the rawhide will end up. Simply run the lacing through these holes back and forth, leaving a spoked wheel up inside the shell. Or you can thread the lacing in the first hole and back out the next hole over, across part of the edge of the head and back in and back out. After you have been all around the drum this way, you will notice half of the edge of the head is pinned down to the shell nicely. To finish the effect, skip a hole on the inside and continue to weave in and out just as before. When this is done, tie off your lacing on the inside of the shell to hide the knot and you are done.

Another option with wooden shells is to drill $3/8$ inch holes and insert pegs into the holes so that they protrude from the shell $1/2$ inch or so. These can be plain or decorative, straight or slightly tapered, but if you know how they quarry stone, you will be careful not to jam the pegs in too tightly, thus splitting the wood. This is easier than you might think and they really do not need to be all that tight, because the stress on them from the pull of the lacings locks them in place quite well. Some drum makers like to drill the holes at a slight angle so that the pegs end up pointing down away from the head slightly. I prefer this method as well, for it assures that the lacing will not pop off the pegs for any reason, and it puts less stress on both the pegs and the shell.

After the pegs are in place, then you can use these to run your lacing around, as in the double-headed technique. A variation of this technique is to drill the holes where they line up with the holes in the shell and peg the head directly to the shell.

.

If you intend to put a simple head on a ceramic shell with straight sides, your options are few. The most common technique is to avoid this kind of a situation. However, if you must, then go all the way down and across the bottom the same way we would for the hoop drum. If you use a metal ring just smaller than the shell's inside diameter on the bottom, you can lace down and around the ring and back up, creating the "V" pattern. This is difficult to do, but you end up with an open bottom, and consequently, a better sound, deeper tone, and a more finished look. The trick here is to tape the ring in place on the bottom of the shell which holds it centered for you while you lace. If you do not use tape, this technique requires a lot of skill to do.

In the case of a ceramic shell that tapers down and gets small toward the bottom, it is easy. Just use a ring, preferably metal, which you can wrap with cloth or leather if you wish. Brass rings which are welded shut are available from most craft stores and come in a variety of sizes. If you are lucky, one of these will fit. If not, you can either wrap the ring with cloth or leather to tighten it up. As long as it snugs up anywhere below the line of the head, it can be practically to the bottom of the shell and still work. If you like to see lacing, this works out all the better.

If you are in a pinch for a metal ring that fits, take ordinary bailing wire and loop it around the shell three times where you want it to be. Then wrap this with cloth or leather to finish it off. Now

you are set. Once you have laced back and forth between the head and the ring, the taper of the shell
prevents the ring from moving. Once again, tape
the ring loosely in place while you are lacing.

Remember, that in all of the lacing techniques
so far, the lacing is complete except for the final
knot before the lacing is pulled tight, which is done
in the same direction and pattern as you originally
laced it.

Repairing ceramic shells is simple. Using fast-
curing epoxy, reassemble the broken piece or pieces,
reconstructing the original shape. Once this has
hardened, apply a thin layer of the same epoxy
over and around the repair area on the inside and
cover this with a piece of cheesecloth or nylon
mesh pressed into the epoxy. This reinforces the
shell and helps the tone of the shell. Give the epoxy
a week to cure; then you are ready to replace the
head or just sit down and play.

So far, in the drum head itself, we have only
been using a simple hole punched in the rawhide.
This works fine, but is only one of many different
ways to treat the edge of the head. A variation of
this is done by punching a second set of holes in the
head 1/4 inch to the outside of the first holes. You
can now place a ring of either metal, lacing or
rawhide under the edge of the drum head. Position
the ring so that it is between the two rows of holes,
and with lacing in hand, begin to fold the edge of
the head up under the ring. Pass the lacing up

under the edge of the head and out towards yourself. This way, the edge is pulled around nicely. If you lace "in and down", the lacing tends to pull the folded edge out of its folds.

With whatever style of lacing you have chosen, continue to finish tying up the drum, repeating the same fold and lace, in and down, until you are ready to pull the lacing tight. This is when you see what a nice edge this can give. You may have to adjust the edge and work out a few folds, but once it is pulled tight, you quickly realize that this edge is much stronger and evenly stretched. The lacing is now pulling against the entire edge of the head and is much less prone to tearing. Metal rings will give you a straight edge around the rim of the head; a lacing or rope will give you a scalloped edge.

The next variation on this theme is the technique of lacing the ring into place around the rim of the head before you tie up the drum. This works better with metal and rope rings which are rigid. Fold the edge under the ring, and begin lacing the ring and the drum head together with a simple spiral stitch, then back again in the opposite direction. Leave the lacing fairly loose, just enough to get the basic shape, and then place the ring and the head on the shell together. Now you can pull the lacing around the ring until it is tight, like tying shoes. Adjust the folded edge as you tighten the laces.

The tricks to this type of edge are many. Using this method allows you to use the punched holes in two ways. You can take the lacing up between the shell and the head, through one of the holes and back down the hole next to it. Or you can pass the lacing down through one of the holes, down to the bottom fastening, whichever you are using, and back up to the rim, down through the hole next to the first, down and back up, through the next hole, etc. Work your way clockwise around the drum in this way.

In the first method, your lacing will be rather parallel lines the length of the shell and will lay flat against the shell, and in the second method your lacing will have the "V" pattern, and will stand out, away from the shell, on half of the laces.

The advantages of this type of rim are an extension of the previous method. You can pull fairly hard on this type of rim without tearing. It allows you a lot of design and decorative choices. But above all, it give the most even tension on the head, topped in this regard only by metal or wooden hardware.

This type of rim is used on all types of drums: tabla/bayan, talking drums, djembé and conga, just to mention a few. So it should be obvious that this type of rim is not only used when you want to put a lot of tension on the heads, even though it definitely has that advantage.

Next, let us look at a lacing technique which involves pulling the laces running lengthwise down the shell into diamond, square, and triangle patterns. This method is not purely decorative, but is used to pull the laces tight and works great if you have a drum with long laces, single or double-headed, that has gone slack and is too loose to play anymore.

The lacing should be long enough to wrap around the drum shell twice. To do this, take a piece of lacing material and tie it onto one of the drum's laces halfway up the length of the shell. Begin by passing over the lace next to the one you have tied onto and over, around, and under the second lace from the one you tied onto. Pass over, around, and under the first lace next to the one you tied onto which is now between the other two. Now pass the lacing you are using under the second lace from the one you tied onto and you have made it. When you have pulled the slack out and the lacing is fairly tight, give it a good pull and the first and second drum lace will cross over each other and should lock your working lacing into place. You should not need to keep tension on the lacing and in fact, you should be able to adjust the cross-over point on the drum laces so that it falls at the midpoint between the two, without the knot coming undone. If it does, just pull it tight again. Continue this method all the way around and tie off your ends.

Formula: over, over, under, over, under, under.

Your drum's tie-up, which was either in the parallel or the "V" pattern, has now become a criss-cross pattern with the crossover point mid-length along the shell. You should notice that the drum straps are now considerably tighter than they were before you pulled them into this new pattern. But let us say your new, or old, drum head has dried and it still is not tight enough to produce a good tone. Do not get discouraged. You now know the best trick in the book when it comes to drum making and you can use it again.

Keep in mind, this special knot works just as well with dry heads as it does with wet heads. If the head is still fairly loose, take another piece of lacing and repeat the same knotting process again. This time, tie your lacing halfway between the top rim and the row of knots you just pulled, one lacing over from your original starting point. This will put your next row of knots a quarter down the length of the shell, and will shift your row of knots, or crossover points, one row over clockwise so that they alternate with your first row of knots.

Continue to pull the straps into their new pattern which will now look like a row of diamond shapes on top of long triangles, when you view the drum from the side. This should do the job in tightening up most loose drum heads. However, if you still have not gotten a good tone from your drum head due to its being loose, repeat the same process just described again, this time toward the bottom. Basically you can repeat this same knotting process over and over until the loose head comes up to the pitch you want.

Some drum makers want this look on their drums, and the heads are applied loosely whether they are wet or dry. This is certainly the method of choice for working with dry rawhide heads, and has an esthetic all its own. With practice, you can predetermine how much slack to leave in the original tie-up, so that you can create any pattern you wish, much like macramé. You can see this type of tie-up most commonly on drums from Africa and the Middle East and occasionally the patterns are very complex. This technique of drum making, however, is used in every part of the world.

Now that you have the drum maker's knot in your bag of tricks, that completes this section on drum heads, so let us take a look now at drum shells.

Almost anything hollow can act as a drum shell. Obviously, you want to avoid anything too fragile. Anything you can mount a head on will work as a drum. (God must have had this is mind when She invented drummers.) You can use wooden barrels, boxes, hoops or ceramic vases, bowls, flower pots, even glass if it is thick enough, such as fish bowls, vases, etc. If you find a vase of ceramic or glass you would like to use, you can take it to your local lapidary shop and for a few dollars have

Wooden dumbek, photograph, D. Kristel, 1995.

them cut off the bottom of the vase and smooth off the edges. This will open up and deepen the tone.

Some very nice drums have been made by combining wooden or ceramic bowls epoxyed to opened-up vase shapes, producing dumbek-shaped drum shells. With two bowls, one glued to each end of the vase you can get some nice double-headed drum shells such as a Talking Drum. If the bowls are different sizes, you have a Chinese or Indian mridangam-type drum shell. Use the double-headed method for tying up and you are set.

Wooden bowls are much easier to work with and are fairly easy to find in the kitchen shops and secondhand shops. You do not need special tools to cut out the bottoms and they take glue and nails very well. Do not try to use the steam-formed wooden bowls, as these are too thin and break or warp. Use bowls that are turned on a lathe.

We have been looking at making smaller hand drums and stick drums so far, but do not forget that all of these methods work for larger drums as well. Half wine barrels from your local nursery and large barrels of all sorts, including aluminum or steel drums can also be used. However, most of these are heavy and involve power tools and a lot of work, but if you are determined I am sure you will figure out how to make them work. One suggestion I will leave you with is to look into PVC tubing, which you can buy in larger diameters from plumbing supply stores. It comes in many thicknesses, and as long as you like. PVC tubing is not too heavy, it is cheap and very workable with simple hand tools. You can combine different shapes and sizes easily and finish off the shell using paint or cloth to produce some very nice drums. Also, it holds up well to rough treatment.

Not all drums have heads of mylar or rawhide. Other types of membranophones have membranes or heads of paper, cloth, and wood. Some drums have heads of fish, snake and stomachs. In this section, I will focus on the first group of membranes. Unless you have access to the second group of substances, it is not worth getting into.

At first when we think of paper drum heads the image that comes to mind is seeing them tear. But not every paper is created equally and rarely is it ever used raw, but acts more as a base for layers of sizing and lacquer. The paper most often used is Japanese rice paper that is lightweight and has a lot of long fibers running at random angles. Actually, this type of rice paper has many similarities to rawhide. It is no accident that the majority of paper-headed drums come from Asia. The East's use of this type of paper combined with masterful lacquer work has produced many fine smaller drums and hoop drums as large as 36 inches in diameter. These are played using a long thin stick across the rim in a similar fashion to the Eskimo walrus stomach drums, thus avoiding tearing the drum head. These drums produce a lot of sound with a wide tonal range, and they are very light.

If you want to try rice paper heads, start by purchasing a stock sheet of quality handmade rice paper of medium weight. The more long fibers the better. Next, you will need some actual lacquer and some thumbtacks. You will also need some water-based artist's sizing. Start by cutting out the paper head so that it overlaps the edge by 1/2 to 3/4 inch. Be sure to look for any weak spots or holes in the paper. Tack the edge down to the shell at one point, pull the paper tightly straight across and tack it down at the opposite point. Now do the same at a right angle to form a cross, then eighths, sixteenths, etc. The method is the same as with rawhide, but the paper is pulled tightly. You can also use glue, either with tacks or not. If you use just glue, use cloth or rubber bands to hold it down, as tape will ruin your paper.

Now apply the sizing as per the instructions that come with it. This will tighten the paper and prepare it for the lacquer. After the sizing has completely dried, you are ready to brush on the lacquer. Work quickly, as you cannot feather the lacquer with your brush. Use even, parallel strokes right across the head. On the second coat of lacquer, make your strokes at right angles to the first. It seldom takes more than two or three coats to do the job and too many coats dull the tone.

The same techniques are used in making cloth drum heads. You can use cotton fabric ranging from bedsheet weight up to thin canvas. The larger drums sound great, hoop drums in particular. Some of these drums get as large as six feet in diameter. As with paper-headed drums, the rim gets most of the play but unlike paper, occasionally the head is struck lightly.

Wooden drum heads have amazing qualities of tonality. They come in every shape and size and are easy to do if you have the tools. The only major obstruction with wooden heads is size and the availability of good hardwoods of the right thickness. If you can find a piece that is wide enough you can have it milled down to 1/4 inch at a lumber store or mill that has a planer large enough. There are both round and square wooden drums.

Finally, I want to describe how Native American water drums are put together. Starting with a deep bowl of clay or metal, size your buckskin, which is soft, tanned and preferably smoked deerskin, so that it overhangs the edge by four inches all around. Soak the skin in water while you fill the bowl with water about one-third of its capacity. Assemble six or eight small marbles or stones and approximately twelve feet of sturdy rope. Now you are set.

Place the buckskin head over the mouth of the bowl and begin to tie the marbles or stones into the buckskin by molding the leather around each marble separately and tying it in place using a short piece of string or cord. The marbles should end up halfway between the bowl's edge and the edge of the skin. An alternative to this is to place the head

Square Wooden Water Drum, photograph and drum,
D. Kristel, 1986.

on the bowl, fold it over the edge and wrap it twice
with your rope to hold it down in place. Now slide
your marbles or stones up under the buckskin and
under one strand of rope, pinning them in between
the two strands. To help hold the stones in place,
crisscross the two strands around the head as you
add each stone.

Tying off one end of your long sturdy rope at the point where the double strands holding the stones cross over each other, run the rope down under the bottom of the bowl and back up the opposite side as you would in tying up a rawhide hoop drum. Run the rope around the double strand at another crossover point between stones and back down. Continue this all the way around and then start pulling the head tight. After you have pulled all of the slack out of the buckskin and the rope, start pulling the rope tie-up very tight. Really put some force into it, pulling it as hard as you can. When this is done, tie off the end of the rope and find a hardwood stick 3/8 of an inch in diameter and the length of your forearm and hand. This will be your drum stick.

To play your water drum, slosh the water in the drum around so that it splashes up on the inside of the head. Now place your mouth on the rim of the bowl so that you can blow air into the drum through the buckskin head. It will inflate slightly and this is what makes the whole thing work. This process has to be repeated occasionally during play.

There is another type of water drum which is simply small bowls turned upside down in larger bowls filled with water. The smaller bowls are then struck either with the fingers or the sticks. The pitch depends on how much air is under the small bowls floating on the surface. The more air, the deeper the pitch and the more resonant the tone.

The real impact of water drums is that the water acts both as an amplifier and a resonator with the water content of the body. Water drums act directly on every cell in the body through resonance. This is why they are primarily used during healing ceremonies and prayer ceremonies. Many aboriginal cultures, including the Native Americans, are open and clear about being able to alter the molecular structure of a body using sound.

Round Glass Water Drum, photograph and drum, D. Kristel, 1988.

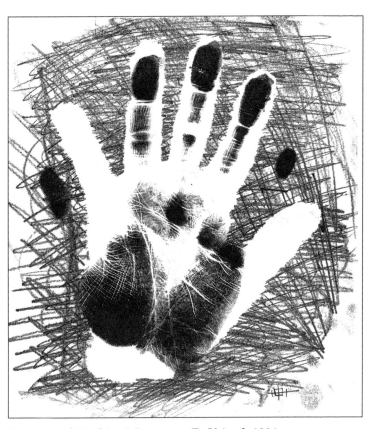

Essence and Machine, Monotype, D. Kristel, 1994.

Chapter Seven

DRUMMING AND MANTRA

I am the Self, O conqueror of sleep,
seated in the hearts of all creatures.
I am the beginning, the middle
and the end of all beings.
        —Bhagavad Gita

In every volume on the subject of drums and/
or drumming (and they are few and far between),
one feature has stood out above all others.

As beautifully illustrated and historically infor-
mative as they may or may not be, they all lack one
basic ingredient. They all address the fact that
drums, in one form or another, have been incorpo-
rated in the life of human beings since anyone can
remember. In this context, years ago I challenged a
friend, a world class historian, to come up with a
time or a place in history in which the drum did not
present itself as a part of that culture. I am still
waiting.

And they address the intimate relationship between the drum and the shamanic practitioners known by many different titles throughout the ages. It is hard to miss the fact that drums have long been used, alone or as part of ritual, magic, ceremony and religion in every culture and civilization of recorded history.

However, subjective speculation aside, they never get closer as to why this is, than to say "something seems to happen" when a certain drum or particular rhythm is played. Aside from reporting on the phenomenal aspects or the results in terms of common consensus language, there seems to be a huge chunk of missing information available for contemporary man to fathom, understand, explain and transmit this understanding to another.

I think this is largely due to a lack of what I call cross-voyaging, by which I mean, beings that are diversified enough in life to be able to put two and two together and come up with five; in other words, beings with a wide enough experiential database combined with scientific information to transcend this mystical barrier in the language of contemporary culture and go beyond the limits imposed on the individual through the practice of legominism, i.e. knowledge and skills passed on through ritual instead of written words.

When it ceases to be mystifying, it becomes pure art.
                                                    —M. Silverwolf

The Great Mystery

The essential self does not have an electrical field,
it is an electrical field.[1]

Drum rhythms set up muscle rhythms which set up breathing rhythms which set up heartbeat rhythms which set up electromagnetic rhythms (this is the "evocational" part) which set up corresponding electromagnetic rhythms in the environment which feedback by reflex to the muscles, to the oxygen, to the blood, to the eliminative and respiratory systems. This reciprocating feedback (this is the "invocational" part), leaves reverberating effects up to 48 to 72 hours after a session.

In other words, from essential self, through the body into the environment, from the environment through the body by reflex, back to the essential self is the whole crux of the process known as self-initiation.

Although sometimes this effect is accompanied by perceptual changes, these are not important. With training, they can be useful as possible indicators of actual changes that are occurring in the electromagnetic atmosphere (third atmosphere) of the biosphere.

The only way essential self can accomplish the adding to, taking away from, or transformation of

---

[1] E.J. Gold, *The Human Biological Machine as a Transformational Apparatus*, Gateways (Nevada City, CA)

itself, is with the use of some sort of medium. One medium is the human biological machine which provides an alternative use of ordinary life.

Short term or long term memory is an almost spontaneous occurrence, and can be viewed as an indelible mark etched upon the fabric of neuromuscular tissue and will remain indefinitely.

Information is held in the body primarily in the deep muscles and is categorized, stored and recalled by the mechanism of the shape of the electrical "charge" placed around an event. Electrical charge and its shape are synonymous. Memories, i.e. specific events and/or clusters of events, are encapsulated within specific electromagnetic fields and act as anomalies within a single event field we commonly refer to as the body.

The body is a thin veneer that interfaces the essential self and the universe. The body is a whole in the fabric of Space/Time.

Essential self interfaces Being with Creation. Essential self can look like anything, take any shape. Any body is a possible vehicle for a fully developed essential self.

The head brain, consciously or unconsciously, places the charge on perceived events, the only continuity being through the mechanism of "persistence of perception." Nerves transcieve, while the muscles store the encapsulated events, much like a food cellar. The shape of the brain affects the shape of the electromagnetic encapsulation matrices. The hands shape the headbrain; therefore, the hands determine the shape of the body and how it functions. Life and work is in our hands.

This encapsulation process also involves a magnetic transfer of a dominant magnetic field over a weaker electromagnetic field: the influence of the machine's field over the essential self. It is these charges and not the actual cellular encapsulation that we are left with after our life in the body, the body having left its mark upon the essential self. What we are actually doing now, and especially how we feel about it, will carry on until the charge downscales through half-life and fades away or is deliberately reformed. It is perfectly possible to alter the shape of the charge around an event cluster without losing or altering the memory of the events which have been stored on a cellular level. It takes substance and force to do this.

One form of "shape-shifting" in the Real World is the process of reforming the shape or charge of the cellular encapsulation around the events within the lifetime. These charges, or more properly, their afterimages, are ordinarily what we are left with after the life within this body. Unlike afterimages, the actual charges around events in which one voluntarily participates remain forever, requiring the waking state as well as a few other basic skills.

When it is okay to remember, we will.

Other **favorite tools used for effecting trans-formational changes** (assuming you have access to a machine in a waking state):

> Myth
> Light
> Dance
> Scent
> Objects
> Circumstance
> Timing
> Anything that produces an evolutionary
>   response from the essential self

Three Basic Elements of the Essential Self:

> Attention
> Presence
> Attitude

Two Basic States of the Human Biological Machine:

> Sleeping
> Waking

The states commonly known as Samsara/Nirvana are associated with the states not so commonly known as Sleeping/Waking.

The essential self, through identifying with the body and all of its illusory, tertiary, so-called "states", falls under the hypnotic effect of the human machine's dominant electromagnetic field. Ironically, it is this dominant effect of one electromagnetic field over the other, that makes the human biological machine the transformational tool that it is. However, this machine known as the organic body, will function as a transformational tool only in the waking state. Sound is a very powerful tool in this respect.

Drumming is a form of mantra or zikr that bypasses the headbrain and requires a whole body participation. This form of mantra does not tolerate mechanicality very well, with immediate observable results if one is "off", and is therefore a powerful tool for invoking one's presence in the present.

Energy goes naturally to the heart when playing music. Headbrain and tailbrain exchange places and the heart center functions as it should. Music is just one way of accomplishing this. Making love, some forms of dance, certain attention exercises and various forms of prayer are just a few.

You could be doing anything and happen on to the waking state. You may or may not be able to hit it again in the same way. You will never forget the experience. If you are successful in achieving the waking state, you may well become addicted to whatever you think it is that produces the side effects of joy, bliss, energy or aliveness (whether or not that activity is appropriate to your station in life or your current circumstances).

This way of turning "upside-down" overrides the primate directives known as the "reticular activator" part of the headbrain, which is consumed with making sense, safety and security. It also bypasses the inherent hesitancy that usually accompanies the misuse of the headbrain. And, yes, you are still able to function. Even better, due to the distinct lack of ordinary conditioning of centers. This is one meaning of "Liberation Through Hearing".

You can see that music is a superb way to go in this respect, if you can see the connection between drumming and breathing and breathing's effect on states of consciousness, and how a musician's life could be a form of yoga.

There are many devices these days which utilize isolation, pulsing lasers, vibromatic water beds and programmed sound, separately or together, to induce a waking state. Unfortunately, not unlike shock or drugs, these systems do it for you and eventually leave the essence weak and immature. There are other natural and gentle methods that are not contingent on this type of technology and require the efforts of the essential self and the body working together.

In ancient shamanic terminology, "It is all right to use assisting factors to open doors, but the day will come when we must pass through those doors on our own efforts." Remember that everything, including states of consciousness, has its own rhythms, and that one of the most important skills gained in drumming with others is the ability to divide and use one's attention, even if you are all allone.

Evolution is always by reflex.

Shakti, photograph, D. Kristel, 1974.

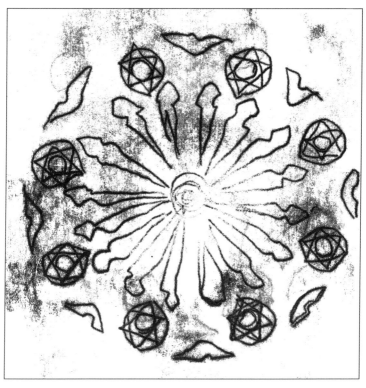

Rose Window, monotype, D. Kristel, 1994.

Chapter Eight

SOUND AND LIGHT

*There is another, eternal nature, which is transcendent
to this manifested and unmanifested matter.
It is supreme and is never annihilated.*
—Bhagavad Gita

A short discussion on the nature and function of light is necessary at this point in order to proceed to the next chapter. This is in no way presented as a treatise, but rather as an introduction for the reader who is without some background on this subject.

Like the old phrase "where there is smoke there is fire", when it comes to light, "where there is electro, there is magnetic". Wherever we find electricity we also find a magnetic field. Wherever we find a magnetic field we also find electricity.

Light in its life cycle, switches back and forth from an electrical state to a magnetic state, each giving rise to the other as it cruises along, pulling itself up by its own bootstraps, so to speak.

You could say that it both destroys itself and by that very act creates itself, and once put into motion will continue indefinitely.

This symbol has long represented light and beautifully illustrates the aforementioned aspects. On one hand, light appears to act like a wave, moving along leaving a wake of offspring made in its own image, expanding out at right angles from the line of trajectory, creating the effect known as hillation. Take note that light's expansion is at right angles from source and is not spherical. However, waves radiate from a source separate from the wave pattern in a spherical fashion and in this respect, light appears to act as a particle generating waves.

Particle or wave? Man, in his ingenuity, has invented a new word to describe this phenomena— "wavicle". As much as this may satisfy some requirements of human intelligence, it brings us little closer to understanding light's true nature and only admits to light's double nature in terms of concept.

The nature of light, it is said, is to be found everywhere and in all things. It is also said that all things emanate from sound. I propose that regardless of which dynamic this electromagnetic plasma manifests itself and regardless of what name we assign to it and regardless of whatever type of apparatus we use to sense and examine it, in and of itself, this plasma remains the same basic stuff of creation. In all of its seemingly infinite varieties, it all comes out of a basic buzz, like in a musical synthesizer where all of the different sounds are generated by and are variations of a single, simple wave form.

This basic buzz manifests as a constant three degree background radiation everywhere in the Universe, permeating and enveloping everything in space. If we can see this, we can begin to understand the true potential in music, to mold and shape the plasma of creation.

When we are playing music we are getting corresponding effects through sympathetic resonance and interference patterns that radiate and influence all of creation, in the act itself and from that point on, the reverberations continue on in one form or another.

Did you know that the sun actually rings like a bell and does so with millions of different wave forms? Did you know that so called "black holes" sound just like Tibetan singing bowls? Did you know that they are both two sides of the same thing, like two sides of a doorway?

Think of the Big Bang as a localized event in an eternal creation, and the true potential of light (and music as a way to shape the light), begins to, as we say, "dawn on one".

For all we know, the Big Bang—a flashpoint of critical mass—is nothing more than a single drum beat.

Maybe God is just a drummer?

We tend to impose biological significance upon electrical phenomena, but the fact is that we are viewing a blue-grey electrical field generated by SOUND.

—E.J. Gold

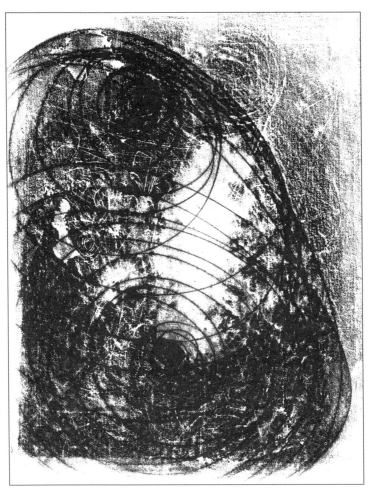

Sound, monotype, D. Kristel, 1994.

Dwapura Upanishad

The mystery of consciousness, this spot of light,
  floating on the soap bubble of existence,
  looking both ways.

Suspended between nothing and eternity,
   wondering, afraid to move;
   for fear of losing yourself in either extreme.
   And lose yourself you will.
For there is no eternity in nothing,
  and there is nothing in eternity.

You have nothing to lose, nothing to gain,
  You are the Tao.
The Tao is one. All things are one.
The Tao of eternity. The eternity of Tao.

The beauty of this mystery is,
  it is always known, known or not.
You can't escape.
You can accept what is;
  what is, will accept you.
Know that this is the completeness of the Tao.
  Zen is the way.
  Tao is.
  Respect. Respect. Respect.

All you can be is what you are.
Even outside yourself, even within yourself.

Your self. Whose self?
Who are you? What is yourself?
      You are Zen, zazen
      The Self is Tao.
The eternal moment;
      now forever, forever now.

Those that see Me as Beauty,
      I will radiate with golden wings of light.
Those that see Me as gross and ugly,
      I will consume in gross ugliness.
Those that fear, shall be feared,
      as those that love, shall be loved
      with My pure loving bliss.
Those that lust,
      shall lust of themselves until consumed.
Those that radiate giving
      shall know no end of receiving from Me.

I am the giver of all. I am the recipient of all.
I give unto Myself, that I may receive unto myself.
I love all that is, for I love myself.
All that be loves Me.

For I am the loving and the loved.
There is no thing that is not of Me.
      Thou art that,
      And I am Thou.

—D. Kristel, 1976

A Slice of the Wheel of Life
(a cross-section)

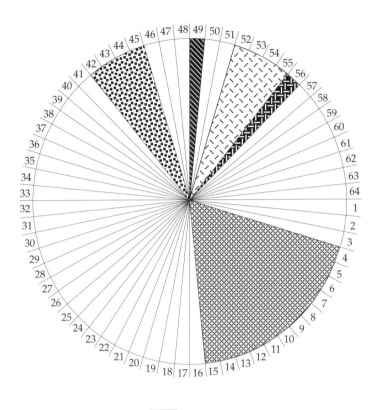

Hearing
Touch
Sight
Taste
Scent

Chapter Nine

THE GREAT WHEEL OF LIFE

If we look at the whole spectrum of the electro-magnetic octaves in a circular form rather than a vertical/linear form, we can easily see the nature of hearing, touch, sight, taste and scent in relationship to the full sixty-four octaves and also in relationship to each other. On a scale of sixty-four octaves (actually septaves, in that each octave is actually composed of seven primary tones) hearing falls roughly within the fourth to the fifteenth range, with the sense of touch on the forty-second to forty-fifth range. The sense of sight shows up on the forty-ninth septave (ironically enough), with the senses of taste and scent showing up in the fifty-second to fifty-fifth, and fifty-sixth respectively. This demonstrates how each of the senses, or "electricities", functions on or within its own range within the whole field of electromagnetic plasma, each separated from the others by a margin of other "invisible" or non-sense-able septaves. This prevents the senses from superimposing or bleeding together. This is determined by the condition of the body and its five level electromagnetic functions. However, this does not preclude the possibility that the machine does have the ability latent within it to sense these missing levels of the whole spectrum.

Using this circular model also allows us to visualize the electromagnetic vibrations as they progress up the scale of septaves to transform from a primarily electric nature to a primarily magnetic nature and at a point of critical mass, at full magnetic potentiality, to reach "flashpoint", and by its own annihilation, switch to its full electrical potential and begin the process again at septave number one. Thus, as each impression or event occurs, the five senses each resonate and absorb their portion.

It could be said that basically we are limited to about one-fifth of the potential of each creation event, each beat of the cosmic drum, each cycle of electromagnetic occurrence. Each dimension has its own rhythm, its own range of vibratory rates. These other dimensions lay within these "missing" septaves, only missing from an apparent lack of sensing.

This demonstrates also that all of the senses are connected through the principal of sympathetic resonance, and in fact, all of the septaves are indirectly connected in this same way. This explains the sensations sometimes experienced, of hearing colors or seeing sound or tasting fragrance, etc. This is a common experience and has nothing to do with mysticism per se.

It should be easy to see from this why all of the major literary works on the nature of Creation, state that all things come from sound, the "Word of God".

Breath is the first motion which leads to sound, the closest sense, the sound becomes light and so on. With this model, creation could be viewed as nothing more than a single event, recurring forever once put into motion, eternal consciousness giving birth to itself forever, at about seventy-thousand cycles a second, and that is only on one dimension.

It really does not matter how you slice the pie. The use of septaves in our model here is merely one way of dividing up the indivisible. One can divide the naturally occurring vibrational progression of octaves, which are figured as twice in number of frequency as the corresponding note in the previous or lower octave and at the same time, half that of its correspondence in the octave above. As Above, So Below. As Below, So Above. And of course, this is occurring on all sixty-four octaves simultaneously. So whether using sound, touch, light, taste or scent to effect some alteration in the atmosphere of the body, all of the senses (and more), on each octave are also being affected. In other words, it really does not matter where you cut in, you will be getting a resonant effect on sixty-three other levels. This also explains why there are side effects which occur unexpectedly.

The octave simply means the halving or doubling of any given frequency, and the range to the resonant correspondent of the chosen frequency: three, six and twelve for example. The halving of the length of a string or the doubling of mass in a percussive object accomplishes this. An octave, however, can be divided into as many pieces as you want. Nor do the pieces have to conform to any specific equal size. As long as the pattern is the same within each octave, the resonant correspondence will be produced.

If, on the other hand, the octaves are individually divided, the correspondences, if any, will not follow any mechanically repeating pattern. In this case, a limitless number of harmonics are available and tonic notes, which sound like a single major frequency can be produced by striking two or more notes simultaneously. However, unlike a single major note which rings primarily on a flat line in pitch, only varying in intensity, harmonics will ring with vibrato, containing within itself the ever changing beat frequency patterns, evolving as the intensity changes throughout the duration of vibration. This kind of tuning is used extensively in Eastern, Middle Eastern and some contemporary music such as the works of John Cage, but is most graphically illustrated in the Balinese music, especially that of the gamalon-gong, which is actually viewed as one instrument made up of many parts. The gongs and bells have been specifically tuned to produce the facsimile of single major notes but are made up of many other frequencies that actually gain in intensity before they diminish and fade out, the various vibration rates reinforcing each other constructively for long after the strike-point of inertial impetus.

Sometimes combinations of notes are used to reinforce each other destructively or cancel each other out, rapidly producing the opposite effect.

Most of this type of music is not designed to be pleasing to the ear but rather to produce exact changes in the listener. In other words, the effects on the body and the consciousness take top priority in the composition.

In its archaic form, this special music of the gamalon-gong was reserved for royalty only. The gamalon-gong was usually set up in a cloistered area off the bed-chambers, separated only by an elaborate grill allowing sound but not sight to enter, and was both a guide to choreography as well as providing the additional force and shocks to assist those inside with the elaborate alchemy of their secret dalliance.

Since the gamalon-gong's resurgence in this century, this has changed. Most instruments were in ruins and the few that remained were being used for ceremonial purposes of other kinds. Although the type or structure of the music is the same, its purpose and function have been dramatically altered and once again, has become largely just another form of entertainment. This type of music usually has the effect on the western ear equivalent to nails being driven through the skull, which is always the case when we superimpose an essence musical form onto the psyche of unsuspecting humans.

Using this circular model and stretching the imagination a little beyond our accustomed limits, we can see at a glance that it provides us with an excellent visual aid to understanding the function of recurrence. In this scenario one's lifetime becomes a great wheel of events in which the past is the future and the future is the past.

> *Singing, I send a voice as I walk.*
> *Singing, I send a voice as I walk.*
> *A sacred hoop I wear as I walk.*
>   —Black Elk[1]

This model of how sound functions could clarify for us the idea of "once done, done always". In it we can see the great Uroborus, and possibly entertain the notion of a psychic's ability to "see the future", which could be just a form of remembering. Even the common phrase "when we forget the past we are destined to repeat it" takes on a whole new meaning. We might even dare to see the Arc of the Covenant as having to do with eternal life, superimposed on our model at the flashpoint of critical mass.

---

[1] From *Black Elk Speaks*, by John G. Niehardt

This leads us inevitably to the processes of recurrence, reincarnation and resurrection, and brings us sooner or later to the School of Music known as

The Way

of the

One Note.

*"I play as few notes as possible, but hopefully they're the **right** notes. The main thing for me is editing—checking out how each note functions in its given place. If I could get away with playing just one note throughout an entire album, I would. When I was sixteen I played faster than I do now, but I wasn't playing anything—just a lot of shit very fast!"*
—Melvin Gibbs
Bassist, Rollins Band
From Bass Player Magazine

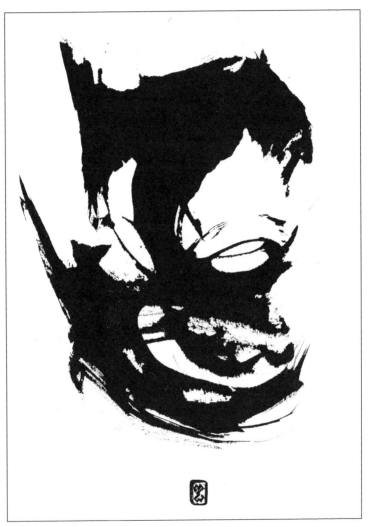

Sumi-e, D. Kristel, 1980.

Chapter Ten

THE WAY OF THE ONE NOTE

The Way of the One Note is an ancient school of music. Not old—ancient. The antithesis of old. Timeless. To refer to this school as old is to try to put it into a time frame. Time is what you learn to transcend in this special school.

Does it teach music? Not in any ordinary way. It teaches sound. Well not exactly sound. It teaches presence but it uses sound to do so. Not exactly sound. Sound as music, sound with presence.

Does it only teach one sound, one note? It teaches that when playing music, in the moment, one is only playing one note. One note at a time. Each note the only note. Making each note with full attention and presence, as if it were the only note.

The school of one note teaches will. It takes will to play a real note, a note with presence. It takes attention to play a real note. It takes the proper attitude to play one note with presence and attention.

The school of one note teaches breathing and walking. It takes breathing and walking to play one real note. It teaches that one cannot step into the same stream twice. One cannot play the same note twice. We are always playing one note even if there are a bunch of them; in the moment of playing, we are actually only playing one note.

The school of one note teaches painting. The way of the one stroke. One is painting one stroke at a time. Our paintings are made of only one stroke. It is called "Cutting The Paper". Each stroke must, as we say, "cut the paper". This means the stroke has force and was made in a moment of freedom. The school teaches how to cut paper with a brush.

The school teaches us to paint on water and to play one note and watch it fade, to overcome our need to cling to the fruits of our labor. Why cling to one note, one stroke? Play another and another and another. No two the same. Each is only one.

When we play the one note we are contemplating the oneness of Creation. When we make the one stroke we are contemplating Eternity. When we play the one note we are not amused. When we brush the one stroke we are not distracted.

The Way of the One Note does not teach elaborate rituals. This would be to try to repeat what we have already done. There is no formula in the Way of One Note. How could there be? As soon as there is formula, the way has been lost. This makes us work each time fresh.

The Way of the One Note teaches us that all things in Creation are interconnected, connected to the one note. One note for one Creation.

The way of one breath. To play the one note it must be played with one breath. This breath must be our only breath. To cut the space it must be our last breath. To cut the paper it must be the only breath. One breath, one life. With each breath we are born, we live, we die and we journey.

One note, one journey. The way of the one note teaches us that there is only one journey, one voyage. How could we travel to the same village twice? Upon our returning the village has changed. It is not the same town, it is not the same road. The people are not the same and the trees have grown. We are always visiting for the first time. We are always leaving for the last time.

We do not know if we will breathe again. We do not know if we will walk again. We do not know if we will visit again. We do not know if we will paint again. We do not know if we will hear again. We do not know.

To a Being who has found The Way of the One Note
playing the same lifetime over and over
is a very viable option.
Recurrence is a very viable option to a Being
able to play in The Way of the One Note.
—M. Silverwolf

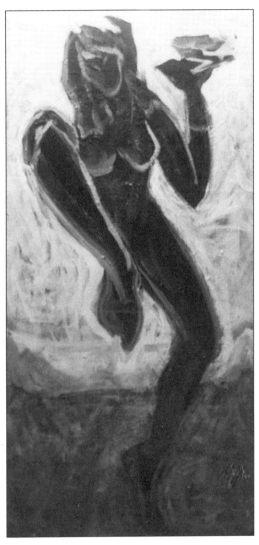

Dakini, Acrylic on canvas, 8″ x 16″,
D. Kristel, 1992.

Chapter Eleven

THE SOUND IT MAKES
IS THE SHAPE IT TAKES

"All structure is created from sound."[1]

Contained in this simple statement is the key to everything this book is about. This kind of statement has been penned again and again in almost every language. In this statement the physicist and the musician can find common ground on which to pursue their studies in the nature of Creation, the same Creation in which we all dwell.

What generates this sound in the first place? Ahkasha: this Sanskrit word is translated as the sound AUM, Pure Space, The Undifferentiated, The Bornless One, eternal motion, Quintessence, the nonphenomenal still point at the center of all other

[1] E.J. Gold, Talk of the Month #28

vibrations and the point into which all things return. Einsteinian physics if I ever heard it.

It would appear then, that Ahkasha has always been around (pun intended). Everything has its arising from it and everything returns back into it, thus generating everything in Creation in an endless stream of raw electromagnetic plasma, which, as it differentiates through ascending and descending vibratory rates, becomes everything we have ever sensed, but are only diffractionating gradients impinging on one another as they find new expression in an infinite variety of electron-space-time-configurations. DNA could be nothing more than a sophisticated tuning-fork.

The word tissue, from the Latin TEXERE, literally means "to weave". What a statement on the structure of the world, its rhythms, periods, cycles, frequencies, serial phenomena, reduplications and sequences. This is the format in which all structures are built and it is ubiquitous. For this activity to remain vital, its whole spectrum should be looked at as a fluctuating entity, and to do this we must develop the view of a moving form and formative movement. This transitional morphology of flux is called "fluid configuration".

Tattva is also a Sanskrit word defined as the mode or modes of motion, the "powers" by which the universe is sustained, and the central impulse which keeps matter in certain vibratory states.

The Tattva cards are sometimes referred to as "skanda" cards. The skandas are the basic elements

of consciousness itself. These five skandas can separate out and recombine themselves into everything sense-able. The world is composed of and we
experience the world through the action of these
five skandas. The skandas are considered to be "the
five fingers of the hand of God".

The Tattva cards have long been used to con-
template these five forces in all of their manifestations and to be able to remember what one has
studied. The body, with its brain, tends to cognize,
store and therefore recall information in the form of
symbols. Alaya consciousness is that which pre-
serves or stores all memories and habits. Also
known as Fundamental or Primordial Consciousness, it becomes the "Wisdom of the Great Mirror".
Memory and learning are made possible because of
this form of consciousness. It is known as the root
of the other forms of consciousness. We live in a
symbolic representation of the world.

The Tattva cards (see Appendix I) are divided
into five groups of five cards each, with a single key
card that symbolizes the origination and dissolu-
tion of the other cards. This card gives the progression of the other cards in their sequence.

Let us start with the first series of five cards
known as the Vesica and are categorized by the
name **Ahkasha**. The Ahkasha series, which have
the common shape of the **pointed arch**, represent
the sense of **Hearing**, and therefore is symbolic of
Sound and the Spirit.

The Skanda/**Consciousness**   The color/**Rainbow**

Next in order is the **Vayu** series, representing the sense of **Touch** and therefore is symbolic of **Motion**. This series of cards has the common shape of the **Circle or Sphere**. The element they represent is that of **Air**.

The Skanda/**Concept**   The color/**Green**

This is followed by the series known as **Tejas**. This series represents the sense of **Sight** and is characterized by the aspect of **Expansion**. The predominate shape here is **Triangular** and is symbolic of the element **Fire**.

The Skanda/**Perception**   The color/**Red**

Next we come to the series known as **Apas**. **Crescent shaped**, this series of images symbolize the sense of **Taste** and the element **Water**.

The Skanda/**Sensation**   The color/**Yellow**

The final set of images are grouped by the name **Prithivi**. This series has the **Square or Cube** as their common shape, symbolize the sense of **Smell**, and represent the element **Earth**.

The Skanda/**Form**   The color/**White**

In relationship to music and drumming in particular, the Tattva images can be used in conjunction with memory. The various rhythmic patterns used in most musical forms found around the world can also be found in the cards. For instance, an entire North Indian classical piece, known as a Raga (meaning a Rag with a beat, the Rag being the ascending and descending notes of a scale and the melody based on that scale) can simply be visualized as one or more of the shapes found in the deck. One can, after acquiring some skill at visualizing, build up an image based on a whole grouping of shapes or track the piece through a series of the cards in varying sequences. As you may have noticed, most forms of classical music from around the world are performed without the aid, or encumbrance, of written music, or scores. It is primarily in the western and European tradition that we find such a heavy emphasis on written music.

For instance, the seemingly complicated rhythms used in playing East Indian raga forms are composed of simple sub-structures based on $3/4$ and $4/4$ rhythms. Occasionally $5/4$, $5/5$, $7/8$, $9/8$ and $11/12$ are used, especially in the "turnarounds", as diverse connectives, and rarely, an entire piece will be based on one of these. However, the all time favorite, is still the 16 beat "teen tal" which is four bars of $4/4$. Good old rock & roll.

Upon first learning the rhythmic patterns, mental counting is used. Besides being difficult, clumsy and distracting, it is also an ineffectual method with respect to long term memory. This type of counting does, however, provide the beginner with the proper training in split attention as well as forging the initial neural/muscular pathways both in the limbs and the brain.

Next comes visualizing the various symbols which correspond to the numeric value of each bar of music. An example of this would be a square representing a $^4/_4$ beat. A triangle is used when playing in a $^3/_4$ mode. When playing patterns involving two rhythmic structures superimposed onto each other, such as three over four, a triangle within a square is visualized with the point of the triangle rotating from one side of the square to the next until the return to the first side, which either keeps repeating or moves on to the next pattern, depending on the structure of the piece being played.

Another example of how three over four is used is this: using a system of twelve beats per section, we can divide this up into four groups of three beats, or three groups of four beats. If we want to start getting a little more complicated, we can divide the measure up like so, 1-2-1/2-2/1-2-1 or we could play it like this, 1-1-1/5/1-2-1. As you can see, the variations are almost endless in appearance and yet are simple to follow if we know the basic underlying structure.

Once these types of training are pretty well established, one moves on to a way of playing which is built on top of the foundation already laid down within the body. This style of playing involves feeling the various patterns with the whole body so that it no longer requires the same mental skill acquired so far and frees up the attention so that it can be placed entirely on "finessing" the music.

Even though I have been using an Eastern/Asian model to express this technique, I think it is important to mention that, it is not uncommon at all to see Western/European musicians playing from memory. They use a rote system to memorize their section of the score, which sets it apart from Indian methods (even though there is a lot of rote memorization involved there, too). The main difference between the two methods is that in most Western music, one just memorizes one's own part, while in most Eastern music one memorizes the entire score with all of the parts. Connected with this difference is whether the piece of music has been committed to memory using a written score or whether the piece has been learned through imaging and orally, either with an instrument or with the voice alone. In the Balinese gamalon and the Indian raga systems for example, the parts are transmitted and memorized using only the voice. Even the drum parts are sung using a special syllable system, similar to the Kototama and Sanskrit, based on the sound that the drums make (for instance Da, Da, Din, Da, Da, Din, Na). And of course, in a Balinese orchestra, a musician could sit in on any of the instruments and play any of the parts.

In Western music, because of the way in which it is learned and played, there is a tendency towards isolation in one's own part and towards a specific orientation to the music based on that part. For example, a violinist paying attention mostly to the violin part, or a pianist focusing mainly on the piano part.

In neurology, this type of attention is called "island attention" because graphically, it resembles an island of high relief surrounded by a moat or depression. In other words, like a high-tech macro lens on a camera, we get a small, highly focused, detailed area known as a focal plane and the rest of the image falls away into a blurry field.

Contrast this with a type of evenly diffused attention which is capable of realizing each of the parts and at the same time, cognizing the entire piece as one whole.

As you can see, the difference in the quality of the music is essentially apparent. What is not so apparent is the quality of the musician. There is a different aspect or being quality that is operative here, for on one hand the "psyche" is being used to motivate and instruct the musician and on the other hand, the "essence" is being used to motivate and instruct the musician. With the psyche, there is a tendency towards the personal and the specific, while with the essence, there is the tendency towards the impersonal and the group.

These two types of being qualities require very different methods and produce radically different results, especially in the realm of the overall harmonious human being and the wisdom, insight and skills that are acquired with it.

OM

The imperishable sound,
  is the seed of all that exists.
The past, the present, the future,
  all are but the unfolding of OM.
And whatever transcends the three realms of time,
  that indeed is the flowering of OM.
This pure Self and OM are as one,
  and the different quarters of the Self
  correspond to OM and its sounds.
                    —Mandukya Upanishad

Visva-Vajra, Leaded Colored Glass, 36" diameter,
D. Kristel, 1972.

APPENDICES

Tattva Cards

Ahkasha Key Card

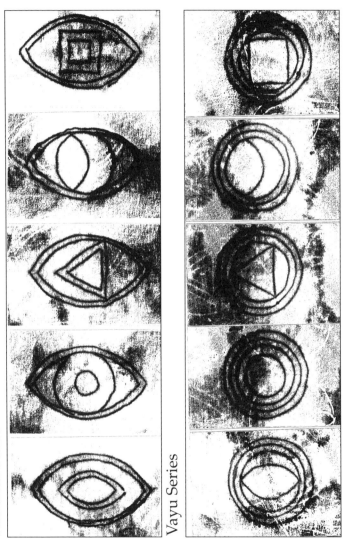

Ahkasha Series

Vayu Series

A4

Tejas Series

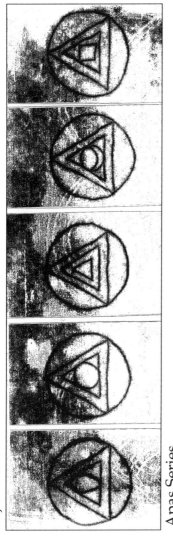

Apas Series

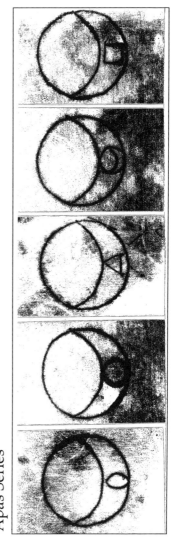

Prithivi Series

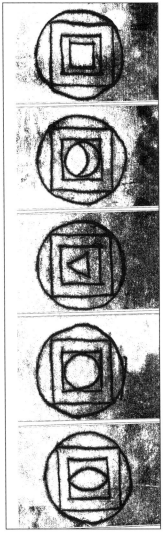

Name	Shape	Sense	Element	Skanda	Color
Ahkasha	Pointed Arch	Hearing	Spirit	Consciousness	Rainbow
Vayu	Circle/Sphere	Touch	Air	Concept	Green
Tejas	Triangular	Sight	Fire	Perception	Red
Apas	Crescent-shaped	Taste	Water	Sensation	Yellow
Prithivi	Square/Cube	Smell	Earth	Form	White

The Guide, Leaded Glass, 36" x 24", D. Kristel, 1979.

Appendix II

THIS UNIVERSE

1. **Absolute** (God) Real Substance
   No name can describe it nor can anything in the creation of darkness or light designate it. This sphere is therefore called "The Nameless", *Anama*.
2. **Holy Spirit** (Eternal Patience)
   It remains forever undisturbed by any limited idea. Unapproachable even by the "Sons of Man" it is called "The Inaccessible", *Agama*.
3. **Sons of Man** (Sphere of Reflection)
   This is where the idea of separate existence of self (ego) originates. This sphere is above the comprehension of anyone in the creation of darkness and is called "The Incomprehensible", *Alakshya*.
4. **Atom** (Beginning of creation of darkness upon which Spirit is reflected)
   This is the connecting link and is the only way between the "spiritual" and the "material" creation and is therefore called "The Door", *Dasamadwara*.
5. **Magnetic Aura** (The Electricities)
   Characterized by the absence of all phenomena, even the organs of sense and their objects, and is called "The Great Vacuum", *Mahasunya*.
6. **Electrical Attributes**
   The presence of fine matter only, all gross matter being entirely absent, and is called "Ordinary Vacuum", *Sunya*.

Appendix III

THE TWENTY-FOUR
ELEMENTS OF CREATION

"..true mastery of the self is mastery of the electrical field of which the self is composed."
—E.J. Gold

* The machine is a five level electrical field.

* The polarized Adam in which the "Son of Man" appears has five electricities. These constitute the Causal Body. Each of these five electricities has three attributes: negative, neutral and positive. In other words, minus one, zero, and plus one, respectively. These three qualities give rise to the objects of sense, organs of action and organs of sense. These fifteen attributes plus Mind and Intelligence constitute the seventeen aspects of the subtle body of the Son Of Man.

* These five electricities, being the causes of all other manifestations are called the Root Causes and are the causal body of the Son Of Man (Purusha). These electricities being evolved from the magnetized/polarized Adam are also polarized as negative, neutral and positive. Negative manifests as the *objects of sense*, Neutral manifests as the *organs of action*, and the Positive manifests as the *organs of sense* and being attracted under the

influence of mind, the opposite of the magne-
tized Adam (heart), constitutes the mental body.

* The aspects of the **negative** polarity (objects of
sense) being combined, produce the idea of gross
matter as solid, liquid, fire, gaseous and spirit.
The aspects of the **neutral** manifest as excretion,
generation, speech, motion and manual skill
(prana). The aspects of the **positive** polarity
manifest as smell, taste, sight, touch and hearing
(in descending order).

* The five forms of matter plus the fifteen attributes
of the five electricities, plus mind (sensing), plus
intelligence (discrimination), plus the heart (feeling), plus the ego (son of man) equals the twenty-four basic elements or principles of Creation
and are sometimes called The Elders.

"These twenty-four principles, which completed the cre-

*ation are only the development
of ignorance, and as this ignorance is composed only of
ideas, creation has no substan-
tial existence but is only a
play of ideas upon the Eternal
Substance of God."*

—Srimat Sri Yukteswar Giri

AMERICAN HERITAGE DICTIONARY

Drum:

1. A percussion instrument consisting of a hollow cylinder or hemisphere with a membrane stretched tightly over one or both ends, played by beating with the hands or sticks.
2. To produce a booming, reverberating sound by beating the wings, as certain birds do.
3. To summon by or as if by beating a drum.
4. To bring about by continuous, persistent effort.
5. To devise or invent.

Drum Memory:

1. A memory device consisting of a rotating metal cylinder with a magnetizable coating on its outer surface, usually used as a nonprogrammable random assess memory. (Computer Science)

Is it pure coincidence that on the same page of almost every American dictionary we find as well as the word "drum", the words, drug, druggy, Druid, drunk, and dry-ad; i.e. wood-nymph?

Appendix V

COLOR AND SOUND

Red..........................397 (G 392)
Orange..................431 (A 440)
Yellow..................464 (A 466)
Lemon....................497 (B 494)
Green......................531 (C 523)
Turquoise..............565 (C 554)
Blue........................598 (D 587)
Indigo....................632 (D 622)
Violet.....................665 (E 659)
Purple*..................565 (A & E 562)
Magenta*..............531 (G & E 525)
Scarlet*..................497 (G & D 501)

* Reversed Polarity

MATERIALS SOURCE LIST

Feather Wand Distributors
Rt 19, Box 90SR
Santa Fe, NM 87505
(505) 983-4011

Gateways Publishing
PO Box 370
Nevada City, CA 95959
(916) 272-0180

Lone Star Percussion
10611 Control Place
Dallas, TX 75238
(214) 340-0835

QX Publishing
PO Box 8415
Santa Fe, NM 87504
(505) 982-3402

Ali Akbar College of Music
215 West End Ave
San Rafael, CA 94901
(415) 454-6264

Zephyr Drum Company
PO Box 22693
Santa Fe, NM 87502-2693
(505) 982-3402

RECOMMENDED LISTENING LIST

Obo Addy
The Rhythm of Which a Chief Walks Gracefully
Earth Beat/ISBN 1-58828-049-4
Distributed Warner Brothers, 1994

Suru Ekeh
Witch Doctor
Eco Art Music, 1992
226 Center Street
San Rafael, CA 94901

Samulnori
Record of Changes
CMP Records, 1988, CMP 3002 CS
PO Box 1129-5166
Kreuzau ER. Germany

E.J. Gold
Ritual of the Cave
Distributed Gateways, HT029, 1989
PO Box 370
Nevada City, CA 95959

Dru Kristel
Where You Are
Distributed Gateways and/or
QX Publishing
PO Box 8415
Santa Fe, NM 87504

Pygmies of the North-East Congo
Music of the Rain Forest
Lyrichord Stereo, LLCT 7157
141 Perry Street
New York, NY 10014

Continuum Percussion Quartet
New World Records, NW 382-2, 1989
701 Seventh Avenue
New York, NY 10036

Bali (Gamelan and Kecak)
Elektra/Nonesuch, 9-79204-2
Explorer Series, 1989
9229 Sunset Boulevard
Los Angeles, CA 90069

Rhythm on Indian Drums
EMI/ CD PSLP 5208

Mamady Keita and Sewa Kan
Fonti Musicali, 1989
ADDA/ 581159

Babatunde Olatunji
Drums of Passion: The Invocation
Rykodisc RCD 10102, 1988
Pickering Wharf, Building C-3G
Salem, MA 01970

Tito Puenté
In Session
Fania, 1994

Scott Fitzgerald
Thunderdrums
World Disc Music/CD M07, 1990
PO Box 2749
Friday Harbor, WA 98250

John Hassel
Dream Theory in Malaysia
EG Records, 1983

Nusrat Fateh Ali Khan
Mustt, Mustt
Real World, 91630-2
9247 Alden Drive
Beverly Hills, CA 90210

The Big Bang
Three CD set, ELLI CD3403
Ellipsis Arts

Geoff Johns
Drum!
Sounds True Catalog, #A-132
735 Walnut Street
Boulder, CO 80302

Zakir Hussain and the Rhythm Experience
Moment Records, Inc.
MRCD 1007, 1991
321 San Anselmo Avenue
San Anselmo, CA 94960

The World of Jegog
Maharani Label - Bali

Appendix VIII

MUSICALLY, ABOUT THE AUTHOR, DRU KRISTEL

Age 4   First record player. Buffalo Gals.
Age 7   First drum. School band. Performances. Classical orchestral percussion.
Age 9   Marching drum for baton-twirling troupe. Performances and parades. Balinese music.
Age 12 First trap set. Keyboards/sousaphone. Jazz, rock and roll. Tito Puenté.
Age 13 First rock band, *The Omegas*. Performances.
Age 14 First J. Hendrix concert. Acid-rock. Second band, *Nameless Uncarved Block*. Performances.
Age 18 First set of tablas. Power-rock-fusion. East Indian classical music. Final belt in Aikido.
Age 19 Tibetan music. Working as rock and roll FM DJ. Apprenticing in leaded glass.
Age 21 Second set of tablas. First sitar. Running weekly East Indian classical radio program.
Age 26 Drumming as essence task.
Age 28 Drumming for *Theatre Absolute*. Performances.
Age 29 Performances in N.Y. Sacred dance.
Age 30 Formed *Not Always North American Drum Core*. Weekly drum, dance gatherings. Performances. Folk, sacred and "bellydance".
Age 32 First solo recording. Performances.

Age 34 First solo album, *Where You Are.*
Performances.
Age 36 Second solo album, *The Wheel.* Performances.
Pow-wow. Resurrect rock and roll.
Age 38 Rock and roll and all the rest from East to
West. Third and fourth solo albums *Quantum X* and *Beat Frequencies.* Performances.
Age 40 Retire from performances. Recording.
Age 42 Band name *Silverwolf.*

In addition to painting, sculpting and designing gardens, Dru works with a small group in New Mexico. A life-time member of the Buffalo Skull Society and an elected member of the Order of the Eagle Feather, Dru spends most of his time in the garden.

QX Publications

Books by Dru Kristel

The Way of the One Note

The Way of the One Note is an ancient school of music, but it doesn't teach music in any ordinary way. Passed on exclusively through oral teachings, the information contained in this small book is the only known written exposition of this special school available in print. Each page is illustrated with an original sumi-e painting by Dru Kristel. Excerpted from *Breath was the First Drummer.*

A Brief History of Music

A real history that begins, not with Medieval music, but with the wind and the music of Creation. Illustrated with images from cultures around the world. Excerpted from *Breath was the First Drummer.*

Garden Beyond Words:

Bonsai • Bonseki• Gardens • Photographs

An exquisitely boxed set of both color and black and white images that conveys the essential beauty of a "little tree" and the hidden meaning of a true garden space.

Watermarks

Written in collaboration with Makundananda Dorje Rinpoche, Watermarks is a *Treatise on Recognizing Clear Light Known as the Great Seal of Void Nature.* This workbook includes a concise exposition of the difference between Tantra and Sutra, and the hidden methods implicit in the Mahamudra teachings.

Music Tapes by Dru Kristel

Where You Are

Performing with Dru on this superbly recorded album is the Santa Fe based Not Always North American Drum Core. A world anthology of percussion, flute, and vocal pieces, this 60-minute tape includes music based on the Native American, Moroccan, Buddhist, and Islamic Traditions. Featured are a variety of ethnic instruments, ranging from the tabla, dumbek, square drum, kudam, flutes, and hammered dulcimer, to the sequencer and synthesizer.

The Wheel

This audio journey around the "medicine wheel" of the ancients takes you to magical places: *Through the Flame, The Land of Native Nothingness*, and *The Gap Between Worlds*. You will meet the First Spirits, the Morning Dove, and the Plant People. The diverse instrumentation also reflects the four directions: Native American drums and love flutes, koto and Shakuhachi, African talking drum, and walrus stomach Eskimo hoop drum are a few of the sounds that will guide you.

Quantum X

The first of a series of private limited editions, this tape features fiery drum set solos as well as whimsical electronic dance tunes. From both a musical and shamanic perspective, the combination of tribal trap drums with live manipulation of sequenced drum tracks draws you into an exciting vortex of energy.

Beat Frequencies
"This album is dedicated to all those who love to speak the language before words." —MSW
The Not Always North American Drum Core—Rah
This collection of live and studio performances demonstrates the unadulterated raw energy of the group. From an ancient/ethnic sound to funk/rap/rock, these archival recordings highlight the diversity of the Drum Core.

Talk Tapes

The Medicine Wheel
An instructional tape that takes you step-by-step through the Medicine Wheel, and how to apply its practice in your daily life.
Slime Mold Technology
Through the adoration and caretaking of these ancient ancestors, we can learn a powerful method of prayer and transformation.
The Cloistered Garden
This tape explores ideas about the cloistered garden as a living example of the Altar and its application to the teachings of the Medicine Wheel.

Videotapes

This video of previously unreleased music of Dru Kristel's includes his virtuoso solos on tablas, African drums, trap drums, bells, gongs, wind instruments and more. With special attention to his breathing and mood, the refined ambience of the space is beautifully captured by Marta Jones.

Books by Martin Silverwolf

Penjing—The Art of Chinese Bonsai
Originally done with handmade brushes of bamboo, yucca, and feather, these graceful and spontaneous pieces of Bonsai trees are printed on richly colored paper.

The Art of Bonsai, Volume II
Black and white reproductions of Sumi-e paintings of Japanese and Western-style Bonsai trees.

The Teachings of the Great Sweet Medicine Wheel
This book is a pondering tool which reflects the multi-dimensional nature of the Medicine Wheel. Each page is a miniature wheel in itself showing a singular dimension of the "Four Directions". Bound by folded rice paper with hand serigraphy, any sheet can be removed and worked with separately.

Faces, Figures, and Other Facsimiles
A handbound collection of reproductions of 56 original charcoal drawings by Martin Silverwolf.

The Shaman Figures of Martin Silverwolf
A full color, hand bound collection of forty-nine reproductions of paintings and monotypes. Mr. Silverwolf's most popular images brought together and assembled into this boxed set are suitable for framing or use as flash cards.

Whistling Fires and Listening Doors
This collection features Martin's haiku—simple and evocative poems based on the Japanese tradition—paired on each page with the whimsical black and white computer graphics of Marta Jones.

Passport: A 17-day Process of Refinement
A passport gives one authorization to pass from a port or leave a country or state. This concise instructional booklet provides assistance on your inner journey by guiding you through a 17-day process that enables you to really observe, reflect on, and refine your attitudes about life.

Recurrents: The Bardo Calendar Game
Conceived by Martin Silverwolf to be used with a Book of the Dead, this unique voyaging tool is designed to help you recognize the macrodimensions by tracking the patterns of the 49-day Bardo cycle.

For further information, write QX Publications, c/o A.D.A.M. Inc., PO Box 8415, Santa Fe, New Mexico 87504, or call (505) 982-3402.

Photograph of author, 1995; Photo Credit: Coleen Rowe